Dear Dick, 10/28/78
Neither you nor the
Red Sox are all washed up!
Keep swingin' and keep the
Faith — Even Yaz
make the most of his young age!
love
Annie
& Joan

THE ILLUSTRATED BOOK OF BASEBALL FOLKLORE

Currier and Ives' "American National Game of Baseball."
(The Museum of the City of New York; Joseph Martin/Scala)

THE ILLUSTRATED BOOK OF BASEBALL FOLKLORE

Tristram Potter Coffin

A Continuum Book
THE SEABURY PRESS • NEW YORK

The Seabury Press
815 Second Avenue
New York, N.Y. 10017

This illustrated edition first published in 1975. Original edition, without illustrations, first published in 1971 as *The Old Ball Game: Baseball in Folklore and Fiction*,

Designed by Anita Duncan
Printed in the United States of America

Library of Congress Cataloging in Publication Data

Coffin, Tristram Potter, 1922-
The illustrated book of baseball folklore.

(A Continuum book)
Published in 1971 under title: The old ball game.
Includes indexes.
1. Baseball—History—United States. I. Title.
GV863.A1C58 1975 398.3′55 75-9968
ISBN 0-8164-9262-X

This book is dedicated to "golden friends I had,"
to Harry Rapakarovitz, Warmette Sands, Hotsi Pototski,
Rathskeller Church III, Val Forge, and the rest,
including Gertie and Walter.

"by brooks too broad for leaping"

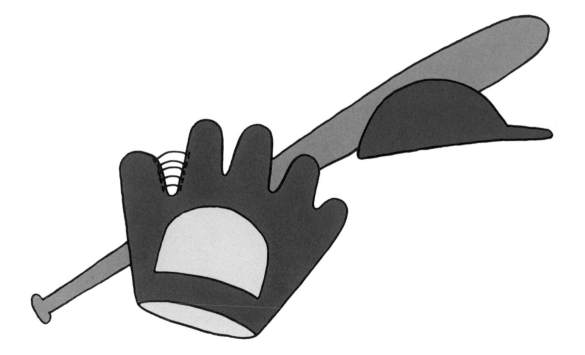

The man who writes a book is invariably a trouble about his home.
It is customary for the author to offer thanks and apologies
to his wife, children, and pets. I do this, too.
Mine certainly deserve as much.

(UPI)

CONTENTS

THE ILLUSTRATED BOOK
OF BASEBALL FOLKLORE

PLAYING BALL.

This 1820 woodcut was prepared
to illustrate a volume called "Children's Amusements."
(New York Public Library)

FIRST

GROUND RULES

Sportswriters argue incessantly whether baseball is the national game or not. On the whole, I think they have decided that it is, but it really doesn't matter. Baseball certainly is one of our national games, evolving to its present forms on these shores, deeply a part of the heritage of our people. The picture of the father shoving a glove and bat into the crib of his first son is an American cliché simply because it symbolizes something typical about American hopes and fears.

Because baseball is so deeply a national game, many people assume automatically that it is a national folk game, or "our great folk game" as it is sometimes called. But calling baseball a folk game is to mis-name it. Much baseball is too highly organized, too set in its rules, actually too literary to be considered folk. Folklore, you see, is the flow of cultural habits, beliefs, ways of expression that a people who can't or don't or won't write use to perpetuate their manner of civilization from generation to generation. It's not much different from the more formal, more highly technological matter that people who write use, except that it is not printed and thus is subject to the laws of oral tradition. That is, it will vary and change as it passes from mouth to mouth, ear to ear, and will not become standardized the way written and printed matter

will. As the folk, who are totally or almost totally illiterate, have no writing, everything they want to pass on from generation to generation has to be passed on orally. People who are literate use writing and printing simply because it is more efficient, lasting, and less subject to accidental variation. Literate people are not folk, and while they may resort to oral tradition to transfer a few aspects of their culture, the fact is they let the bulk of the work, the really important work, be performed by the printed page. The library and the university, not the tale-tellers or the singers of songs, are the "keepers of their culture."

Therefore, the first law for calling something folk is to make certain that it is being passed along orally as part of the perpetuation of a culture. Organized baseball, the game played in the schools and colleges, by the American Legion teams, in the Majors, with its highly complex set of rules and techniques, has to resort to writing to endure, changing only when there is a conscious, studied agreement to cause change. If it were a folk game, it would survive as hop-scotch or ball-bouncing survive on the playgrounds, simply because one group of people teach it to another, varying from group to group, area to area as participants forget, misunderstand, or get caught up in fads that enter

Former Dodger great Jackie Robinson gives a few pointers to his son, Jackie Jr., and Little League teammates in Stamford, Connecticut in the spring of 1957. *(Wide World)*

it. Baseball where it is less formally played, where unpoliced, casually coached, is a folk game. When it is played as "one old cat" or "monkey move up," when it is played with five kids to a side on some sandlot, when it is softball at a picnic, when it is stickball, it is a folk game—each one a variant of "folk baseball," each played with a set of rules that are generally agreed upon, but subject to spontaneous variation. But "organized baseball" is

not this breed of "old cat." It is as literary as a textbook, and no matter how many millions of people play and watch it, no matter how much television exposure it gets, it remains a product of our sophisticated, not our folk, culture.

Thus, one must keep the terms "folk baseball" (what I will call "folk-ball" where I use it) and "organized baseball" (what I will mean by "baseball" from now on) separate. Most people don't bother, but I must. For this book is not about folk-ball. It is about organized hardball baseball, in two parts. The first five chapters will concern themselves with organized ball as an occupation and with the folklore that develops in and about that occupation. The last three chapters will concern themselves with organized ball as a subject or backdrop for all sorts of journalists and authors during the last 100-odd years. To be sure there is a good book to be written about folk-ball. Maybe someday I'll try to write it, but I am not trying to write it now!

*   *   *

Like most things, organized baseball wasn't "invented" by anyone: it evolved. There is a legend that Abner Doubleday started it all in 1839 when he was a cadet at the United States Military Academy. Supposedly, he laid out the first diamond in a cow-pasture at Cooperstown, New York, where he had once been a student at Green's Select School—and from that moment on baseball existed. Although the legend has long since been discredited, people like to go on believing it the way they believe Washington heaved a dollar across the Rappahannock or Lincoln

walked three miles to give back 6¼ cents he had over-
charged a customer. Cooperstown, New York, was chosen as
the spot for the National Baseball Museum and the Baseball Hall of Fame, and every year two major league teams
play a symbolic contest at Cooperstown to honor an event
that never was. For there is no excitement in evolution,
and even less in the idea that America's national game is
rooted in English antecedents. Man seeks a dramatic
moment when some doctor nails a peach basket to the
running track above the gym floor, when some undis-
ciplined player picks up the football and runs with it.
Abner Doubleday will do. At least he is both definite and
patriotic.

**Major General Abner Doubleday, popularly credited with
toeing out the first baseball diamond with the tip of his
well-polished shoe as a West Point cadet in 1839.** *(New
York Public Library)*

**Alexander Cartwright, who systematized baseball
ground rules in 1845 and helped form the New York
Knickerbockers baseball club.** *(New York Public Library)*

The National Baseball Hall of Fame and Museum in Cooperstown, New York, hosts thousands of visitors annually. (Wide World)

Obviously, organized baseball is derived from the British game of rounders, with its bases, fielders, feeder (pitcher), its "ins" and "outs," its need for open spaces. In fact, forms of rounders were referred to as baseball or postball long before America was settled. Alice Bertha Gomme, at the conclusion of her description of rounders in Volume II of *Traditional Games of England, Scotland, and Ireland* remarks with true British dispatch:

An elaborate form of this game has become the national game of the United States.

Colonial versions of rounders were apt to be casual. One variant that became popular was called "one hole catapult" or in slang "one old cat." In this variation, the batter struck the ball with a stick, after which he ran to a stake or base. He scored if he could get back "home" again without being soaked (struck) with the ball. In most versions, he stayed at bat until he was soaked or until someone caught his hit on the fly. When a batter was put out, each fielder moved up a position toward his turn at the plate. If a fielder caught a ball on the fly, he exchanged positions with the batter at once. When there were enough people, two stakes were provided and the game was called "two old cat." In towns, where a lot of people got together of an evening, three stakes were used, four or more men were put to bat, the rest sent out to field, and the name of the game was "town ball." The pitcher wanted the batter to hit, for that was the only way in which the others got their chance, and usually there was no such thing as a foul. Anyone who has played bean-bag on the beach or "monkey move up" with a tennis ball has little trouble understanding the matter. In fact, when someone "gets up" one of these impromptu contests at an outing or after supper, sketching out the ground rules as the game starts, he is doing exactly what his Anglo-American ancestors were doing in true folk fashion generations before.

By the early 1800s, forms of town ball had become a popular means of working out village-to-village rivalries, and the element of "sides" was strong in it. Just as the highly trained stick-fighters of Trinidad crowed their

The New York Knickerbockers team, organized in 1845, was the first regular baseball club to be established in New York. *(New York Public Library)*

1845
THE FIRST
ORGANISED
BASEBALL CLUB

kalinda and represented their yard against the champion of the next yard, just as the jazz bands of New Orleans tried to outplay the jazz bands from the next district over, so the best ballplayers were pitted one against the other with local pride and a good bit of money hanging in the balance. Most of the games, like most of the stick-fights and music contests, ended up in brawls. This is because stick-fighting and music contests and town ball all represent semi-civilized replacements for village-to-village wars. And this is an aspect of the game that has never left it. In September 1967, work in four huge American cities, Chicago, Boston, Minneapolis–St. Paul, and Detroit, approached sheer inefficiency as the local franchises battled down to the wire for the American League pennant. During the final two games of the season, when Boston amazingly defeated Minnesota to win it all, a number of classes were suspended at such an unlikely place as Wellesley College so that girls who barely knew where Carl Yastrzemski would run after hitting the ball could take rapt part in this modern village-to-village crisis.

But town ball, like a true folk game, lacked codification and in many cases disputes over the rules generated more feeling than the contest itself. Folk-ball needed Ten Commandments and a Moses to publish forth the tablets. Alexander Cartwright, 6′ 2″, over 200 pounds, proved to be this prophet. In the spring of 1845, he systematized some ideas he and his friends had been tossing around for several years. He regulated the bases. Instead of arranging them casually or in the U-pattern used by many New Englanders, he set four of them in a perfect square each 90 feet from the other, placing the batter at home. Instead of using posts or stakes or rocks, he used flat bases. At each one he stationed a player, putting one specifically at the active spot between second and third and calling him the shortstop. He limited the total number of players to nine on a side, allowing but three in the outfield, and he insisted that the batters bat in a regular rotation to be announced before the match began. He eliminated the idea of soaking the baserunner with the ball for an out and instituted the idea that the hitters and fielders would change places after every three outs rather than after the whole team had been retired. However, he did not set the number of innings at nine. Under Cartwright's rules, the final inning was the one in which a team went over 21 aces (runs).

Cartwright's ideas tightened up the game of town ball. The rapid flow of innings increased spectator interest, throwing to a base or tagging a man for an out eliminated a lot of time wasted chasing balls, while the set positions for the players proved both defensively sound and enabled specialists to develop. With the firmly established rules, teams from various areas could meet each other fairly and without wrangle. It was inevitable that Cartwright's commandments became gospel. Town ball players had long been ripe for indoctrination.

The first game worthy of being called baseball as we think of it was thus played at an appropriate spot, the Elysian Fields, in the inappropriate town of Hoboken, New Jersey, on June 19, 1846. Cartwright, a teller in the Union Bank on Wall Street, was a prosperous young sportsman. His ball-playing friends were men of similar background, mostly involved with finance, and they established a club of gentlemen amateurs to play the newly codified rules. Their association, called the Knickerbockers,

**The New York Knickerbockers (left) and the Brooklyn Excelsiors (right)
in 1858, separated by a top-hatted umpire. These teams,
two of the earliest organized ballclubs, were among a total
of 25 American clubs formed by 1858.** *(New York Public Library)*

lost their first outing 23-1 to a group called the New York Club, with Cartwright acting as umpire. From 1846 on the new rules spread rapidly, and in 1860 a tour by the Excelsior Baseball Club of Brooklyn did much to popularize what was then known as "the New York game" up and down the Eastern seaboard from Washington to New England.

At first, as with cricket, a "baseball match" was a social occasion. Tea was served, the ladies were invited, gentlemanly conduct on the part of the contestants prevailed. As the idea was to let the batter hit, the pitcher threw the ball where the batter requested. Bunting was an inexcusable breach of taste. Players trapped off base politely permitted themselves to be tagged out, and phrases like "nicely bowled, sir" were simply adapted to the new game. But in America it couldn't last. Democracy, introduced into the game by gambling, reared its ill-bred head. As more and more money began to change hands, clubs began to look for better and better performers, often reaching well down the social ladder to obtain them. These new players, good as they were, had little idea of the British code of gentlemanly sports. They bunted, dodged on the

This 1869 lithograph portrays
the Cincinnati Red Stockings
of that year.
The Red Stockings' pitcher,
Mr. Brainard, is featured at center,
sporting luxuriant side-whiskers.
(New York Public Library)

basepaths, threw the batters any pitch but the one requested, even shouted at the opposition. And they won, so the bettor found little reason to look askance at their *parvenu* means to his competitive end. In addition, the Civil War broke out, and "the New York game" was introduced to the Union and then the Confederate troops, sweeping like dysentery through the Army camps, down the South Atlantic coast, and out into the Midwest. By the time the wounds of the nation were bandaged, Cartwright's game was the most popular game in the land, freed from the rich, property of all.

As the popularity of the sport continued to mushroom, it became expedient to form a national organization, the National Association of Baseball Players. In it, the issue of amateurism (gentlemanism) and professionalism raged much as it has done in the lawn tennis world of the 1960s and early 1970s. For although all the clubs claimed to be made up of "amateurs"—a nuance derived from their common "Knickerbocker" ancestry—the larger ones made no bones about hiring outstanding players. And the competition for the good ones was as keen and unscrupulous as it is today in "shamateur" college basketball and football circles.

Professional and amateur players didn't mix socially off the field. Their relationship was much like that of the professional and gentleman jockeys of the "hunt club" horse-racing circuit. Sometimes, in order to lend a certain respectability to the hired players, they were given token jobs with the businesses run by the gentleman players. Like a southwestern football star, they might never show up at these jobs, merely let their names appear on the payroll, and thus create the illusion they were being paid for services other than those of the diamond.

In such a situation, the step to outright professionalism is never long in being taken, and by 1869, only 24 years after Cartwright "published forth his tablets," a professional baseball team was formed. It was the Cincinnati Red Stockings and came about through a very natural evolution. In July 1866, Aaron B. Champion, a well-known lawyer, joined a few of his gentleman friends in starting a typical amateur group to play baseball. They leased the grounds of the Union Cricket Club and soon had lured most of the cricket players and most of the fans away from

This gigantic championship bat was presented to the Cincinnati Red Stockings by some of the city's leading citizens when the ball club returned from its season's tour in 1869. *(Culver Pictures, Inc.)*

the English game. One of the cricketeers was the Britisher, Harry Wright. Though he had played "the New York game" for years, Wright was working for the UCC as a cricket bowler at a salary of $1200 per season. However, when he saw how popular baseball was becoming, he went to Champion with the idea of a frankly professional team. Champion was willing, and the Red Stockings were formed. By March of 1869, they were ready to play, with ten players, including Harry's brother George, under contract.

The new team started out by defeating a number of local teams and then embarked on an eastern tour to challenge the established clubs. They won ten games en route to New York and on June 14 scored an impressive 4–2 win over the Mutuals in Brooklyn. They went to Washington, were received by President Grant, and, excepting a five-inning tie in Troy, New York, managed to remain unbeaten for somewhere between 57 and 65 games. During the season, which didn't close until November 5, they travelled almost 12,000 miles by rail and boat, played before 200,000 spectators on both coasts, and even showed a profit of $1.39 on the venture.

The Red Stockings were not beaten until one year to the day after they "established" themselves against the Mutuals. On June 14, 1870, after opening the season with 26 straight wins, they were upset 8–7 in 11 innings by the Atlantics before a crowd of about 20,000 in Brooklyn. They lost five more that season, and then disbanded in September. Wright moved on to Boston, taking the name Red Stockings with him. Today both the Cincinnati Reds and the Boston Red Sox continue tribute to what was both the first and surely the most nearly invincible professional club ever assembled.

In 1871, the concept of outright professionalism was widely enough established that Wright and some others felt free to break away from the National Association of Baseball Players and found the pointedly named National Association of Professional Baseball Players. This can satisfactorily be termed the first major league, though it wasn't until the formation of the National League of Baseball Clubs in 1876 that set schedules were used and the franchises were run like businesses. The switch in stress from a loose association of players to the business organization caused the need for the reserve clause which was introduced in 1879 to keep players from jumping from team to team. By 1883, another professional league had begun, the American Association, and a "World Series" was conceived. In 1890, the players, fed up with salary limits and owner tyranny, formed their own league. The result was twelve years of greed, struggle, and instability that nearly destroyed professional ball. However, in 1902, the old National League, which had survived, and the Western League, now called the American, came to an agreement which has lasted to the present. Thus, transcendent above franchise shifts, expansion, division play, television exploitation, and reserve-clause problems, baseball has stood a reassuring beacon of stability for the twentieth century.

As I have said before, it matters little whether the old "New York game" is now our national game or not. One thing is certain, it has gained a remarkable hold on the American public during its "baker's century" of existence. It has proved itself to be an unusually stable game, needing few major rule changes, satisfying though played day after day, sufficiently complex to fascinate the poet,

Union officers and enlisted men mingle with prisoners of war during a baseball game at a North Carolina prison camp, 1862.
(New York Public Library)

Thomas Eakins' "Baseball Players Practicing, 1875." *(New York Public Library)*

sufficiently obvious to please the peasant. It offers a more sensitive balance of physical skill, problem solving, and chance than any game I know. It is hard to play well, yet easy to learn. It is fun to watch, yet challenging to study. It offers excellent patterns for gambling. And its popularity has grown steadily abroad, in lands as disparate as Japan, Central America, and Canada.

Throughout its history it has been identified with our "manifest destiny." After the Civil War, when baseball was formulating, America needed a national game, as well as national heroes, legends, and literature, to shore up its pride, soothe its self-consciousness, and explain its attitudes to established European and Asian cultures. The same need that created Abe Lincoln of Illinois, Hale in the Bush, Paul Revere's Ride, fostered the idea that baseball heroism was second only to military and political heroism, that good fathers must play catch with their sons, that professional athletes are keepers of the national morality, that the World Series is a seasonal rite. Nor is there much wrong in all this. Nations, people, children need stars to which to hitch their wagons.

A large part of the hold that organized baseball has on the American imagination derives from the concept of loyalty to the franchise rather than to the individuals. In a world fast reeling from the rural to the urban, in a country where one does not live where he grew up, in the ever-changing megalopolis, loyalty to a baseball franchise offers the same assurance and stability that "home for the holidays" does. So the Braves move from Boston to Milwaukee to Atlanta, so Wally Berger, Eddie Mathews, Orlando Cepeda come and go, the voice of Fred Hoy still sounds across the years to the fifty-year-old Los Angeles lawyer as he re-lives his Medford, Massachusetts, youth during a 1969 pennant drive.

If one gets into an argument whether or not organized baseball is the national game, it is the intensity of this old village-to-village feeling that will strike the most telling blows for baseball. Try as they may, none of the other professional sports has been able to "get to" a city the way major league baseball does during a tight pennant race. Perhaps it is because of the long identification baseball has established with our way of life, more likely it is because of the day-by-day nature of the game. Regardless, the community homogeneity that a pennant race can engender is truly a mass phenomenon, usually overriding ethnic differences, lack of interests in sports, certainly overriding common sense.

Joe Falls, Sports Editor of the Detroit *Free Press,* had a fine column on this point in *The Sporting News* of October 26, 1968.

Riot Scars Still Visible

My town, as you know, had the worst riot in our nation's history in the summer of 1967, and it left scars which may never fully heal. More lives were lost, more property was damaged, more people were hurt—more pride was wounded—than in any of the other civil disorders.

And so, as 1968 dawned and we all started thinking ahead to the hot summer nights in Detroit, the mood of our city was taut. It was apprehensive. It was fearful. You even heard talk that Detroit was becoming an armed camp. The night that Martin Luther King was gunned down on that balcony of his motel in Memphis, more people in Detroit probably thought about buying firearms than at any time in the history of the city.

When Lyndon Johnson announced he would not run again for President, the tension mounted, and it became almost intolerable on that frightening morning when we all saw Robert Kennedy cut down in that kitchen pantry in Los Angeles.

They were awful days—truly awful. Nobody was quite sure what would happen. Everyone seemed to fear the worst. And the newspapermen of Detroit were helpless to do anything—to expose the false rumors, if nothing else—because our strike droned on and on.

But then something started happening in the middle of 1968. You could pull up to a light at the corner of Clairmount and 12th, which was the hub of last year's riot, and the guy in the next car would have his radio turned up: ". . . McLain looks in for the sign, he's set— here's the pitch . . ."

Somehow the street corners didn't seem as crowded, especially when the Tigers were playing on TV.

Or you could walk along the sands of Metropolitan Beach and there'd be so many portable radios around that you'd never miss a pitch.

The bumper stickers started to appear: "Sockit to 'em Tigers," "Go Get 'Em, Tigers," "Tigertown, U.S.A."

Some of these would be pasted on one side of the bumper, next to the ones which said: "I have a dream."

And downtown, in the Corktown section at Michigan and Trumbull, the lights burned brightly and the place rocked and reeled from the cheers of another crowd of 40,000.

The City Found an Outlet

This was a baseball team trying to win a pennant. Men playing a boy's game. Pretty silly when you stop to analyze it. Especially when you thought of the boys who were losing their lives in Vietnam.

But my city needed a release; it needed an outlet to release its pent-up emotions. It found it in a baseball team, men playing a boy's game.

Willie Horton is colored. It didn't matter. Did you see the one he hammered off Kaat last night? People who were prejudiced to the center of their souls found themselves rooting like mad for the Willie Hortons . . . and the Gates Browns . . . and the Al Kalines . . . and the Mickey Stanleys . . . and the Denny McLains.

The fans nearly tore the Stadium down the night the Tigers clinched the pennant—their first pennant in 23 years—and then they nearly tore the town down the night they won the World Series.

I wasn't on hand for the second celebration. I got stuck in St. Louis writing stories for my paper. It's a nasty habit I've gotten into. But they tell me it was really something.

The people on our block, where Mickey Stanley lives, went wild with joy. I called home and my wife was weeping—she was so happy. They decorated The Mick's house and celebrated until four o'clock in the morning.

Some Ugly Incidents

Downtown the mood was festive at first, then it got ugly. Two men were found shot the next morning, one girl was attacked in the middle of a park. Looters took advantage of the situation and ransacked stores.

But these incidents—cruel as it may sound—were minor compared to the unrestrained happiness which spread throughout the rest of the city. I grieve when I think of the shameful incidents but these happen

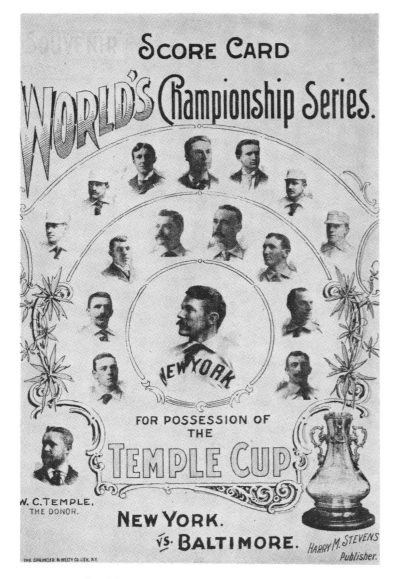

A scorecard sold at an 1890s Temple Cup game. The annual Temple Cup championship series was a forerunner of the World Series. *(New York Public Library)*

in every city of our land. Really, it was nothing compared with the joy of thousands . . . even millions . . . of others.

It made you think. Why were these people so happy? Because a ball team won a championship? That's part of it. But I can't believe it's all of it.

I believe that they wanted to express their hope . . . a belief that life is good, and can be good, under the proper circumstances. They used a baseball team as a way to express these emotions and while baseball may be a sick game, as *Newsweek* Magazine alleges, I don't think any other sport could have turned my town on the way the Tigers did this summer.

It was a year when an entire community, an entire city, was caught up in a wild, wonderful frenzy. For a moment, even I forgot some of my worries.

Nor is what Falls described unique. It happens almost every year in one or two cities across the nation. I mentioned earlier the phenomenon as it affected Boston in 1967; the same thing went on in Chicago and New York in 1969, as the Cubs and the Mets fought through September for the division championship. On the 31st of August, when the ill-fated Cubs appeared to be home free, D. J. R. Bruckner of the Los Angeles *Times* News Service wrote these lines,

The whole city is a bit insane. Old ladies sit in parks holding transistors, with earplugs stuck into their ears, like teenagers. The effect can be wild: You walk along and suddenly see three or four old people with plugs in their ears jump off their park benches cheering. You do not know what has happened, but you can guess. A judge in Criminal Court ejected a spectator from the courtroom when he noticed the man was frowning and smiling secretly to himself, and that there was a tell-tale wire running from his ear down under his shirt collar.

People on subways who have never met, look at one another, frown, shake their heads, and pass on. No need for talk.

And on October 17, 1969, after the Mets beat the Cubs, the Braves, and the Orioles to become World Champions, Frederick H. Treesh wrote for the UPI,

From Fifth av. to Wall st., from Flushing to Staten Island, it was all one big happy party.

Confetti and computer cards littered Manhattan's streets and sidewalks. Toilet paper festooned skyscrapers.

New Yorkers on buses and subways were talking to each other—an oddity. A Bikinied barmaid near Grand Central station was pouring gin into martinis with reckless abandon.

New York, the big city, was just as small—and just as enthusiastic—as anyplace else when it came up winners.

Anyone who has lived in the United States during a twentieth-century summer knows the intensity and catholicity that such passages describe. Perhaps more remarkable, then, is the steady tendency during the last decade to disparage and downgrade baseball. Where once the voices chanted steady denial that our so-called national game might have originated with the British, now the chorus joins in proclaiming that baseball is too "old hat" to be our national game, too slow, too mired in the past, not violent enough for fast-paced modern minds. And all this while 35 million people a year are passing through the turnstiles of professional ballparks, while Little League, Babe Ruth League, American Legion and college ball are flourishing as never before, and while softball, stickball, and variants of "one old cat" are being played in the cool of every summer evening.

Much of the chanting comes from sportswriters and mass-media people, and it is baffling stuff if thought about logically. For example, the argument that the game is too slow for the times can't make much sense when golf, which takes longer and in which there is almost no action at all, has become bigger and bigger as a spectator sport. In fact, it is almost axiomatic that the man who finds baseball a bore is a golf buff. For a while I thought the continual anti-baseball chorus might be trained and paid for by professional football entrepreneurs who were hoping to build one game by tearing down another—and I do think this has happened to some degree. It has also occurred to me that some of the discontent may stem from the night game which traps the reporter in the press box deep into

Manager Stallings and his Boston Braves on the bench, 1914. The Braves' franchise moved from Boston to Milwaukee to Atlanta in later years. *(New York Public Library)*

the wee hours. It is natural for a reporter to prefer a game that ends at a set time and to be impatient when a contest, particularly a routine one, drags on and on. Likewise, television people prefer contests that end predictably as baseball never can. More than once I have got the impression that the TV industry would be delighted should the American public lose all appetite for such indeterminate entertainments. But these reasons can't be more than superficial ones. There is so much money to be made from baseball, one finds it hard to believe that promoters, newsmen, television men, even the players themselves are trying to maim or kill a goose that is still laying golden eggs. More likely, I think, the downgrading of baseball is a form of national flagellation, brought on in mid-century by our discontent with our imperial policies and domestic situation. I think we feel, unconsciously, that the American way of life is not working out exactly as it should, that greed, bias, industrialization, and militarism have eroded the glory that was America, and that we attack baseball, one of our national symbols, as part of the "establishment," as we are attacking our class system, our sex mores, our educational system, the WASPs, the Defense Department, the Presidents. Paradoxically, I believe that the more criticism chanted against baseball the more the evidence that it is after all our national game, immigrating with us in the eighteenth century, becoming American with us during the nineteenth century, vilified by us as we regret the twentieth.

Thus, although organized baseball is not a folk game, it is a century-old, national phenomenon influenced by and influencing our culture. The people who play organized ball, sometimes starting their careers in folk ball and entering organized baseball at the American Legion or minor league level, form a well-established occupational group, and as an occupational group they possess a certain homogeneity that separates them from others who earn their livelihood in different ways. Consequently, while organized baseball is not a folk game, the people who play organized ball form a group that has many of the characteristics of a folk group, does develop a heritage of beliefs, customs, tales, and proverbs that perpetuates occupational standards, that serves to include and exclude individuals.

As participants in the occupations often rely heavily on physical prowess, nerve, native intelligence, as well as on thorough training, for success, the homogeneity of such groups is likely to build itself around these qualities, developing a lore that offers model behavior patterns. Will James, discussing the cowpoke of two generations ago, stresses the significance of being labelled a "top hand" in Chapter 7 of his novel, *Sand*:

That was it, being a hand. Laughing when there's danger and hardships, laughing when there's danger of getting a leg, or neck, broke, the same as laughing when stinging sleet stiffens the muscles and makes laughing hard to do. That's all in the making of a hand, a principle which every cowboy does his best to live up to.

It's the cowboy's religion, and living up to it makes him of a breed that's all his own. With that it already takes a certain breed of man to make a cowboy. That breed might be found anywhere so long as it's stirred and the start is early enough, but as a rule that breed grows up right in the heart of the cow country, and the true cowboy, even tho he knows of many other ways of living that are soft, will always be a cowboy. He won't care if his wages are low so long as the ponies are rough and the country is big.

Joe Garagiola tries to get at similar things in his chapter "Between the Foul Lines" in *Baseball Is a Funny Game*.

You cross the white lines onto the field of action and find the air thick and tough to breathe. The mound makes you a sitting duck. The ball weighs a ton. The distance to home plate seems to be farther than to the center field flagpole. You are a midget pitching to Superman. The hitter is on top of you, and the double deck stands are tumbling down. Now how do you perform between the foul lines?

or,

. . . He knocks you down, and you don't like it, but it's you or him. He slides hard on the double play, down you go, but you don't let him beat you getting up. It's you or him. He's going to bowl you over to score that run. Brace yourself, and don't rub when you get up. It's you or him. You can't call for help, and you can't go home. You don't like it, but it's you or him. Run and you are through. To some the air gets thicker now, the bat isn't long enough, and the pitcher is too close. This is the beginning of the end. Others go down to the dirt but come up with the flashing thought. "I've got to battle back." This is the end of the beginning.

Of course, the cowboy lives in such a way that he really does have to risk his neck in order to remain a "top hand" in the eyes of his peers; ballplayers don't have to go that far. But if enough publicity is focussed upon them, if enough money hangs in the balance, a ballplayer can find himself in a position where he must prove himself almost as if his life were on the line. Ask Ralph Branca, whose pitch enabled Bobby Thomson to win the 1951 pennant for the New York Giants; ask Felix Mantilla, whose fielding lapse gave the 1959 pennant to the Los Angeles Dodgers. If people care enough, the pressures can be intense.

But failure is not a sin. Ralph Branca and Felix Mantilla were "professionals," "top hands," in the eyes of the other ballplayers—and they tried. They did their job, did their

New York Mets manager Gil Hodges and his wife are inundated with confetti thrown by jubilant New Yorkers during "Met Day" ticker tape parade in Lower Manhattan following the Amazin's' 1969 World Series victory. (Wide World)

best, and failed only because someone has to fail when a decision has to be reached. The sin is what Joseph Conrad describes in *The Secret Sharer*, the failure of a member of the group to conduct himself according to the laws of the group. Conrad's story depends on the fact that you can't blame Leggett, a sailor, for killing a man whose insolence endangers the group. The success, the survival, of the group depends on the adherence of the members to the code

Fireworks explode over the
field as the diamond
is overrun by delirious fans
joining the Oakland "A"s
in celebrating their 1974
World Series—clinching
3–2 victory over the
Los Angeles Dodgers.
(Wide World)

of the occupation, to the homogeneity of the occupation. And the lore: the legends, the songs, the superstitions, the customs that develop in the occupation are designed to emphasize and re-emphasize the behavior patterns so that none can forget them.

Surely it would be wrong to push the similarities of organized baseball to cowpunching and seafaring too far. Organized baseball is not a full-fledged folk occupation in the sense that cowpunching or following the sea one hundred years ago were full-fledged folk occupations. For example, the sailor of the mid-nineteenth century lived out his whole life on and about ships. He seldom saw people whose interests were different from his own. He had no radio, television, or even books to introduce him to other points of view, other interests. To him, to his family, the sea was everything, and without education, often without literacy at all, he simply learned what sailors before him had learned, preserved these attitudes while he flourished, and passed the profession and the lore that held things in focus on to the youngsters, dying utterly parochial, narrow, and folk: as Nathaniel Hawthorne wrote, "retiring from the quarter-deck to the homestead, while a boy of fourteen took the hereditary place before the mast."

There are three qualities that define such genuine folk groups. One is that they possess an intense homogeneity built on occupational, regional, or ethnic isolation. Two is that the literature, the lore, which is used to perpetuate the code of this homogeneity, be passed on not by writing and print, but by word of mouth, so that it will continually vary and change, never establishing itself in a definitive form as printed matter does. And three that this lore be the mainstream literature of the group. Thus, in a true folk

occupation, one learns what he has to know both as a member of the group and as a member of the human race by means of oral literature and oral literature alone. It is all he has.

Yesterday there were many genuine folk groups: sailors, cowhands, lumbermen, hill farmers, slaves, hunters who lived as occupational, regional, and sometimes ethnic folk groups in America, fused together under one national government, but isolated from one another by ignorance and their parochialism. Today, America has changed. Today, we have established, somewhat artificially, a single national heritage into which we try to educate all our people with a steady stream of propaganda from swaddling clothes to winding sheet. By means of schooling, mass media, and rapid transit we have broken down the isolation of the old occupational, regional, and ethnic islands and given each and all a pre-digested, packaged national lore that supplements and often replaces the individual folk heritages of the past. The result is that where one hundred years ago an occupation like seafaring was a genuine folk occupation, now it is what you might call a "semi-folk occupation," with a "9 to 5" homogeneity that gives the participants an individual identity while at work, but a homelife that is indistinguishable from the homelife of persons in other semi-folk occupations like nursing, factory work, or baseball. No longer must the son take "the hereditary place before the mast." The avenues that lead from today's seas are broad, well-marked, and many. He is educated to walk them.

In a semi-folk occupation the lore is, on the whole, confined to the occupational portion of a man's life, and while it tells him what it is to be a member of the group, he learns

Four ten-year-olds go after a pop fly with vastly different approaches
after applying for precedent-setting entry into the Elmhurst
Baseball League of Evanston, Illinois. *(Wide World)*

President Woodrow Wilson
seems to share his audience's
delight as he tosses out
the first ball
of the 1915 season.
(New York Public Library)

what it is to be a member of the nation and of the human race through printed matter and the mass-media outlets that he shares with Americans involved in a variety of occupations, whose homes are far-flung, whose ethnic backgrounds are polyglot. Baseball players live in such a way, for while they share the homogeneity and lore of their occupation during much of the day, even on a road-trip for a couple of weeks at a time, they do not carry this homogeneity or lore into their homelives, into the lives of their children or wives, as a true member of a folk group must. Their homelives they share with all other Americans, with the butcher, the baker, and the maker of candlesticks.

These, then, are the ground rules. Your job is to keep them in focus as you read about the lore and fiction of one semi-folk occupation, organized hardball baseball. Mine is to restrain myself from writing, "Batter up!"

Brooklyn Dodger Jackie Robinson steals home as Giant Wes Westrum sprawls across the plate in a futile effort to tag him in the second inning of a 1956 game at the Polo Grounds. *(Wide World)*

SECOND

THE FOLKLORE OF BASEBALL

AT the very beginning, when baseball was a gentleman's game, most of the participants were well-educated Anglo-Saxons, what today we might call WASPS. As the game went professional and drew from the lower social orders, it was dominated by the Irish and the Germans. This was the situation from the 1870s to the First World War. After that struggle to end all struggles, a large number of Italians and Poles entered the game and were joined there by a lot of southern and southwestern rural Anglo-Americans. As soon as Jackie Robinson was permitted to break the color-line in 1946, American Negroes flocked into organized ball, soon followed by Spanish-speaking Islanders, Central and South Americans, both Black and White.

These rough patterns were predictable. Baseball, like all professional sports, is an outlet for the underprivileged. It is too risky to appeal to persons with good educational and economic opportunities, and one can see, as each group betters itself, a falling off in the number of its ballplayers. There are not many Germans in baseball today; fewer Irish, fewer Italians than there were. As the Blacks improve their situation, there will be fewer American Negroes, and eventually, perhaps, the game will be dominated by the Latins and the Japanese. The number of rural Americans must dwindle, too, as towns crop up and educational opportunities improve in the outlands.

The White ethnic groups that have fed ballplayers out of the city ghettos are numerous. However, it matters little whether the people involved are Germans, Irish, Poles, or Italians, the pattern is always the same. The man and his wife come to these shores broke, lured by opportunity. They go to work in menial jobs, at hard labor, in factories. The women, confined to the home, see little of their new land and establish a Little Hamburg, a Little Dublin, a Little Milano for their men to come home to at night. Their native tongue, or dialect, remains their main language. The old peasant ways and lore are not disturbed too much by the trans-oceanic trip. However, the children are forced to go to school. In a short time, they think of English as their native tongue, may well speak the old tongue or dialect, but are aware of the obvious discrimination peasant ways and Old World habits bring them. They marry, often to members of other ethnic pockets. They make money. They emerge and acculturate. Their children and grandchildren are Americans through and through, don't know or care about the old ways, may well change their names. Baseball, if it is to serve such people at all, will serve them in the second generation, in the third, but seldom longer than that.

Although such ethnics may be resented by the rural Americans, especially those from the south and southwest, country people are of the same color, are often of similar

25

"Choosing Up"—a 1910 illustration by P. V. E. Ivory depicts neighborhood youths choosing up teams for a spring diamond contest. *(New York Public Library)*

racial stock, and are certainly undergoing similar experiences in acculturation. For as they move from the rural to the urban, they too are tossing aside old, peasant ways; feeling embarrassment over their backgrounds; learning to act and even speak like people who make up the bourgeois flow of American, urban life. It is the old American phenomenon of the immigrant boy or country boy making good in the city, learning that his background is best discarded or modified. The result is that streams of folklore that might be flowing swollen into an occupation like baseball are not only drying up at the sources, but are being dammed by the reluctance of the participants to stress their backgrounds.

The Black American does not move as decisively away from his folk background as does the rural or ethnic White who enters baseball. There is discrimination in the locker room as well as upon the streets, and the Black tends to stick to his own to a far greater degree than the White who finds it relatively easy to move among other Whites of different nationality and of different regions. What's more, the distinction between the rural Black and the city Black is scarcely demarked. Even if a Black is from a northern or western ghetto, he is not far removed from the rural South, the chances being that his parents moved north or west between 1915 and 1946 and that he still has relatives there. Consequently, all American Blacks share a common heritage which, along with their common problems, makes them less embarrassed by the old ways, the old tales, songs, and beliefs. Thus, the Blacks do carry more of their home culture to work, although, because of discrimination, and the Spanish-language barrier, they do not share it readily.

The Latins, whether Colored or White, are of course

isolated by a language barrier which in many cases is almost complete. Products of a world where distinctions between Blacks and Whites are nowhere near as crucial as they are in the United States, these players are frequently from rural Caribbean backgrounds that are almost completely folk. Unlike the bulk of the American Black and White players, some of them are close to illiteracy—if not in their own cases at least in those of their families. Many of them know a great deal of lore that a folk collector would be anxious to hear, but they do not contribute this lore to the English-speaking players who are so foreign to them. Language barriers, color barriers, separate them from the White ethnics and White rurals. Language barriers, religious barriers, separate them from the American Blacks.

Thus, although one might think baseball folklore to be melded from the contributions of its polyglot peoples, a tale here, a proverb there, a superstition there appealing to all ballplayers and surviving to shore up the codes of the group, things are just not that romantic. Ballplayers, while fused by the homogeneity of their profession and sometimes by the intensity of the common goal of winning, are still "9 to 5" ballplayers. From "5 to 9," as it were, their backgrounds reassert themselves and fragment that homogeneity. Thus, the Harlem Black, the Georgia Cracker, and the Cuban Creole may be close at the ballpark, perhaps even on the road, may hug and kiss each other, fight for each other in the heat of the game, but they have little in common once they go home.

Under such circumstances, it is difficult for a significant amount of folk material brought into the occupation to spread through it and be universally meaningful to the

W. W. Denslow created this 1909 portrayal of a self-satisfied "Casey at the Bat" dressed in quilted baseball togs and a bewreathed cap—clearly prior to the legendary strike-out immortalized in Ernest L. Thayer's famous poem. *(New York Public Library)*

members. For instance, think about the story of the revenuers who bribe the small boy to show them the way to his
daddy's still. When he asks for the money before they
leave, the revenuers tell him he'll get it when they come
back. He replies, "No, I won't. You ain't comin' back!"
This tale means one thing to the southern hillbilly who has
seen revenuers killed, quite another to the urban Italian
who thinks revenuers are characters out of old *Esquire* cartoons or to the Dominican who doesn't really know what
revenuers are at all. Likewise, a Georgia Black and a
Georgia Cracker will look somewhat differently on the
anecdote about the Northerner who gets off the train in the
Southern town and asks the station-master, "Where do the
colored folks around here hang out?", only to be told, "We
usually hang them out down there in that clump of wil-
lows." Nor can either the American Black or the White
fully appreciate the tale about the Mexican who thinks
Americans are referring to a man named Juan José when
they keep replying "Wha' you say?" to his questions. A
story must be quite generalized to appeal on the same level
to all ballplayers, with the result that the game, which is
the common meeting ground of the players, is also the
common subject of practically all of their lore.

Obviously there will not be any major forms of folktale
or folksong in this lore. The reason is simple. The role
played by the ballad, the spiritual, the lyric song, the myth,
and the legend in a folk community is provided by the
main culture. There is no need for the ballad, the spiritual,
the lyric song in a "9 to 5" occupation where the music of
the radio, the church, and the juke-box is available. Nor
does baseball as an occupation lend itself to work songs.
In occupations where work songs are functional, for pulling

ropes on foggy decks, for keeping restless cattle from stam-
peding, they will develop, although today's electricity and
radio make them less important than they once were.

Baseball players don't have myths for similar reasons.
Myths are tales that are essentially religious, explanatory
in nature. They are believed by the teller and the listener.
They reveal how the world got to be the way it is, why men
live the way they live, why there is fire or sex or death or
the accepted code of ethics. Ballplayers, living in a Chris-
tian-Hebraic culture, don't need myths. The main culture
provides such things through Roman Catholicism, Protes-
tantism, Judaism, Mohammedism. In a society such as ours
even full-fledged occupational groups, like buckaroos and
seafarers, don't have myths. They too get their religion
from the main culture. And it is misleading to talk of the
"myth" of Captain Kidd, of Jesse James, of Babe Ruth or
Willie Mays. Such figures are heroes of legends, not of
religio-explanatory tales.

Legends are folk and popular history. They are tales
that are also believed, but which deal with events that happened or should have happened to men and women who
have lived in the world created and ordered in the manner
described by myths. Legends take place, as it were, "this
side of myths," in what I have sometimes called "the touch-
able past." They offer examples for people in the present
to emulate and hold up standards of behavior that the culture feels it must maintain. Full-blown, historical legends
do not develop among ballplayers. They and their families,
and their "after-hour" friends, are not illiterate. They have
been to school in the main culture and absorbed as history
the written legends of the American people. Nonetheless,
like most occupational groups, ballplayers have an urge

Baltimore Oriole shortstop Mark Belanger autographs baseballs for young hometown fans during a break in the 1970 World Series.
(Wide World)

Bat Day, an annual promotional event at Yankee Stadium for fans under fifteen years of age, made a big hit with these youngsters, who received bats at the Yankees-Twins doubleheader in June, 1965.
(Wide World)

Miss Margaret Miller of Oakland, California, leaves no room for doubt as to whom she's rooting for as she arrives for the 1973 World Series opener between the Oakland Athletics and the New York Mets. *(Wide World)*

Spring can't come too soon when your throwing arm is itching for action and a new glove is begging to be broken in. *(New York Public Library)* toward history, and they will develop embryonic legends that offer models for professional conduct.

Legend, then, is the only major form of folklore in the heritage of ballplayers. However, there will be a wealth of minor, folk-literary forms: a lot of jokes; many superstitions and beliefs; a host of customs; a few proverbs, proverbial sayings, and truisms; and a cant—all working to maintain the homogeneity and ideals of a life separated "by the foul lines" from the main culture. Let's turn to legend first.

The most famous baseball story of all is the legend of Babe Ruth's home run in the 1932 World Series. The historical setting was the fourth inning of the third game between the Chicago Cubs and the New York Yankees. The Cub bench had been giving Ruth a terrible riding, paying particular attention to his lack of a family tree. He had already hit one homer when he came to bat against Charlie Root in the top of the fifth, so the Cubs really let him have it. When Ruth swung and missed the first pitch, he held up one finger for the yelling crowd and the bench jockeys to see. After the second strike, he held up two fingers amid deafening jeers and hollers. Root then "wasted" a couple trying to get the Babe to "go fishing." The count was quickly reaching a showdown. "At this point," Paul Gallico remarks in *His Majesty the King*, "Ruth made the most marvelous and impudent gesture I have ever seen. With his forefinger extended he pointed to the flagpole in centerfield, the farthest point removed from the plate." When Root's fifth pitch disappeared over that very centerfield wall, right beside the flagpole, needless to say it did so before a hushed and literally amazed crowd.

The story is so well known that people who care little about the game have heard it, and generally, as legend should, it has come to be accepted as true. God alone knows whether it is true or not. Everyone knows that Ruth held up his fingers indicating the count as it went from one strike to two. Everyone knows that the booing became intense and that two balls intervened. Everyone knows that Ruth extended one finger just before Root released the historic pitch. It is of no account whether he was actually pointing to the flagpole where he was to hit the ball, whether he was wiping his eye, or whether he was indicating he still had one swing left. Legend demands that he was pointing, or legend doesn't exist. Root, who was certainly there, gave his version of the matter in a speech to a Los Angeles high school assembly.

Sure, Babe gestured to me. We had been riding him, calling him "Grandpop" and kidding him about not getting to be manager of the Yankees. We wanted to get him mad, and he was when he came to bat. As he stepped up, he challenged me to lay the ball in. After I had gotten the first strike over, Babe pointed to me and yelled, "That's only one strike."

Maybe I had a smug grin on my face after he took the second strike. Babe stepped out of the box again, pointed his finger in my direction and yelled, "You still need one more, kid."

I guess I should have wasted the next pitch, and I thought Ruth figured I would, too. I decided to try to cross him and came in with it. The ball was gone as soon as Ruth swung. It never occurred to me then that the people in the stands would think he had been pointing to the bleachers. But that's the way it was.

Any ball player, even the cockiest, would be pressing his luck to call a homer at 2 and 2 against a pitcher like Charlie Root, even if he knew what Root was going to throw. And Ruth would have had to have been a complete nut to select the flagpole in centerfield, the most distant

Young Brooklyn Dodger fans demonstrate in a 1957 effort to "Keep the Dodgers in Brooklyn." The Dodgers moved to Los Angeles' Wrigley Field despite the vociferous protests of loyal Brooklynites who wanted their Dodgers to continue to call Ebbets Field home.
(Wide World)

reach of the park. To answer boos by calling such a shot is incredible. To answer boos by wiping one's eye is unlikely. To answer boos by holding up a finger to indicate "You still have one to go, kid" is reality. But what chance does reality have? Paul Gallico has written that Ruth's homer "warmed my heart and made it glow beyond all cynicism." Eyewitness, umpire George Magerkurth, who worked the '32 Series, has said, "My biggest thrill was when Ruth hit that 'indicator' home run." There can be no other explanation for the raised finger. Thus glory makes her transit of earth, else man would have no past.

Baseball's legends are seldom as stable as the one about the "indicator home run." The vignettes that ballplayers use to keep the virtues and vices of their occupation in focus are usually but motifs, quickly sketching nerve, bravado, eccentricity, indifference, cowardice, integrity, or some other characteristic to be honored or scorned. Attached for a time to a well-known, if somewhat faceless hero, they are ever free to move as reputations flow and ebb. Typical is the story of the pitcher who calls in the outfield and proceeds to strike out the side. This motif is presently linked to Rube Waddell who did it in 1904 when with the Philadelphia Athletics. He was pitching against Cleveland with a 1–0 lead. The bases, and possibly Waddell, were loaded at the time. Surely the trick had been

Babe Ruth watches his record-breaking 60th season homer sail up and away during a 1927 Yankees-Senators contest. The Babe set the record in a 154-game season. Roger Maris slammed 61 homers in a 162-game season in 1961. *(Wide World)*

tried before 1904, at least in folk ball. As Waddell's reputation has waned, the story has gravitated to other pitchers of more current fame. Recently, I heard the tale told about Satchel Paige, who seems to have tried it when the fancy struck him in barnstorming days.

There are literally hundreds of such motifs in circulation. A batter yells at the pitcher, "You're so mean you would low-bridge your own mother!" and the pitcher replies, "Yeah, but Ma was a pretty good hitter!" A pitcher walks over to the opposing dugout before the game and announces that he is throwing nothing but fastballs that day and then goes on to twirl a one-, a two-, a three-hitter. A batter tells both the pitcher and the catcher that he is going to bunt, steal second, perhaps third and home, then does it. A spitball is so wet it sprays the batter's face as it goes by. A fastballer is so quick he gets strikeouts without throwing the ball, his catcher simply slapping the glove three times, fooling batter, umpire, and fans. A famous catcher meets a former player in the elevator and doesn't recall his name but remembers he can't hit low, outside fastballs. A batter stands in the batter's box staring at a new model plane passing overhead and is called out on three straight strikes. A star pitcher remains sober before the crucial game and loses, while the manager curses himself for not letting the guy get drunk.

Anyone who has been around baseball can go on and on. For the moment, these anecdotes have their particular "faceless hero": Early Wynn, Dizzy Dean, Ty Cobb or Jackie Robinson, Burleigh Grimes or Gaylord Perry, Walter Johnson or Bob Feller, Bill Dickey and Joe Gantenbein, Zeke Bonura, Ellis Kinder. In fact, some wander so rapidly from hero to hero that we think of them as "just anecdotes" that happened to no one in particular. Who was the rookie who wired home from spring training, "Put another cup of water in the soup, Ma, they started throwing curves today"? Who was the slugger who promised to "hit one" for the sick kid? Who was the player who got thrown out of the game because he told the umpire he was sick, sick of bad calls? Who was the catcher whose handshake was like holding a bag of peanuts, walnuts, cashews?

On the other hand, clusters of anecdotes may group themselves about a particularly representative figure and through their accumulation perpetuate his personality. This means, of course, that a genuine folk hero is beginning to emerge. The phenomenon is inevitable in all homogeneous groups, and baseball began to develop its legendary heroes with their cycles of petty adventures almost at once. One of the earliest was Michael Joseph "King" Kelly. Quick of wit, self-indulgent, careless, carefree, sentimental, generous, alcoholic, the mustachioed Kelly was the darling of baseball fans in the '80s and early '90s when the game was still young and the rules were still lax. He played any position, sober or drunk, cheated, clowned, excelled. One of the first players to make base-stealing an art, he packed the impoverished Irish immigrants into the stands to see him light out for second, fake the' fielder, hook the bag, then rise to crow and wave at the happy fans. His daring made the cry, "Slide, Kelly, Slide," into a household phrase, inspiring his pal, monologuist John W. Kelly, to compose a satiric song under that title. He played vaudeville, endorsed cigars, opened a saloon, and demanded huge salaries for the era. As Celtic as Mrs. Murphy's pig, he dressed like a Blarney-kissed *boulevardier* with a tall hat cocked over one eye, jaunty clothes, and shiny high-buttoned shoes.

The Kelly legends center on his opportunism and his

"easy-go" tricks. Sure and it is King Kell who drops his mask in the third-baseline to hamper a runner about to slide on a close play at the plate, who realizes that a right-fielder can grab a hard-hit liner and throw a slow runner out at first, who sneaks fifteen feet inside second or third to take an extra base when the solitary umpire's back is turned. And 'tis Kelly who takes advantage of the rule that allows a substitute to enter the game at any time by simply notifying the umpire. In Boston, he leaps from his spot on the bench shouting, "Kelly now catching" and grabs a foul fly which his regular catcher was not going to reach. And one day, as the sun starts to set in the last of the 12th in Chicago, he pulls the grandest stunt of all. Playing right-field with two out and the bases full, he leaps into the twilight trying to catch what "has to be" the game-winning homer. As he comes down, he holds his glove high above his head, and jogs cockily toward the dugout. The umpire yells, "Out number three! Game called on account of darkness!" "Nice catch, Kell," his teammates shout as they slap him on the back and ruffle his handsome hair. "Not at all, at all," Kelly roars back. " 'Twent a mile above me head!"

King Kelly eventually drank himself out of the big time. At 37, he was dead, victim of pneumonia complicated by high living. Still, he goes out with "last words" worthy of any hero. Taken semi-conscious from the New York boat to Boston Emergency Hospital, he slips from the stretcher on which he is being carried to the corridor floor, quipping, "I think, me lads, this is me last slide!"

It is difficult to distinguish such embryonic legendary matter from the simple gag or joke. The Honus Wagner tale about the dog who grabs the grounder forcing the shortstop to throw both animal and ball to his thirdbaseman who tags the sliding runner with the whole confused

package is clearly "Joe Miller" material, as are the "rubber chicken" anecdotes of Lefty Gomez: the one about Bill Dickey's telling him to throw harder and getting the reply, "I'm throwing as hard as I ever did, they just aren't getting there as fast," or the one about Frank Crosetti's yelling, "Bear down, Lefty, the sacks are loaded" and getting the

Babe Ruth is greeted by Lou Gehrig (#4) and Joe Sewell (#21) as he chugs into home plate after driving in two runs with a homer in the first inning of the first game of the 1932 World Series. *(UPI)*

reply, "I know they're loaded; I know I don't have two infields behind me." But is it possible to distinguish between such gags and the anecdote about Burleigh Grimes' spitter which sprays the batter's face or Walter Johnson's catcher who can steal strikeouts by merely slapping his glove three times? Perhaps the real distinction has to center on the function of the material in the occupation. Legendary matter is believed by the narrator and listener; it records and instructs. Jokes are not believed, and have no other purpose than getting laughs.

Clearly legendary are the tales that concern the way in which major league franchises got their names, though such matters are of little concern to the players themselves. Joseph G. Gephart, writing in the New York *Times Magazine* section of February 23, 1941, catalogued a large number. Reading over his article, one has to have doubts about the historicity of quite a few. It seems most unlikely that the St. Louis Cardinals were really named in 1900 by an unknown lady who saw the red-trimmed gray uniforms and gushed, "Isn't that the loveliest shade of cardinal!", nor can I believe that the Cleveland Indians are so called because a group of them acted like savages at a party thrown by James C. Dunn. On the other hand, it is true that the Dodgers got their name because Manhattanites derided Brooklynites by calling them "trolley dodgers" and in spite of all efforts to replace that name with Superbas, Kings, and even Robins during Wilbert Robinson's tenure. It is also true that the Pirates got their name for signing a star, Louis Bierbauer, who in 1890 jumped the American Association for the outlaw Players League. Bierbauer had originally been with the Philadelphia Athletics. When the Players League folded he should have returned to the A's,

but they forgot to include him on their lists and Pittsburgh signed him up. There were protests, but to no avail, and when one of the Philadelphia papers referred to the affair as "an act of piracy on the high seas" a name was born. Since then Pittsburgh has been the Pirates or the Bucs (Buccaneers). Furthermore, the New York franchise became the Yankees when the names Hilltoppers and Highlanders proved too cumbersome for news coverage, and the Tigers did get their name from the old blue and orange striped sox they once wore. However, whether blue and orange stripes reminded people of Princeton's orange and black and then the tiger or the tiger directly must remain moot.

As with the Robins of Brooklyn, some names just can't be made to catch on. The Boston Bees were named by a blue-ribbon committee of baseball writers from a choice of about 1300 ideas, but the team, though now in Atlanta via Milwaukee, is still the Braves. The Philadelphia Athletics, labelled a "white elephant" by John McGraw when Ben Shibe purchased them, never really became the White Elephants, although the team was long identified by an albino pachyderm and did use the jibe as a nickname for a number of years. The Phillies wanted to become the Blue Jays, but they are still the Phils. The Cincinnati Reds, hoping to avoid identification with Communism, tried to become the Redlegs with but moderate success, and the Colt .45 people forced the Houston expansion team to give up ideas of being the Colts (once the name of the Cubs) by being legally difficult. Naturally, each time a franchise moves its name comes in jeopardy. The Boston Braves and the Philadelphia Athletics have retained their names in Milwaukee and Atlanta, in Kansas City and Oakland, respectively, but the St. Louis Browns had to become the Orioles, a traditional Baltimore name, when they moved.

As the players are indifferent to how their teams were named, such legends must be considered peripheral to the folklore of baseball. They are the concern of sportswriters and club publicists, men close to the dugout but not quite a part of it, men who will be our chief concern later in the book. Superstitions, on the other hand, are important to all ballplayers.

Religion is a formal set of beliefs used to explain the unknown to man, used to comfort him in time of stress, used to keep his ethics in focus, held together by a mythology. Superstition, as best I can define it, is any belief that lies outside the framework of one's formal religion. Thus, if one is agnostic or atheistic, all religion and all beliefs of that sort are superstition. If one is Christian, pagan religions are made up of superstition, and so forth. For years I have used the following anecdote to show what I mean. A Negro ballplayer in South Carolina left his family and ran off with the beautiful wife of a friend. The ballplayer's wife immediately went to the Baptist minister and asked him to pray to God that her husband be punished for his sins. The minister complied. Meanwhile, the friend went to a voodoo doctor and requested the same thing, that the man who ran off with his wife be punished. Shortly after, the sinner tried to break up a double play and broke his leg instead, so badly that he never played ball again. Both wronged parties felt that divine intervention had wreaked its vengeance. Which one is superstitious, which religious? It simply depends whether or not you believe in voodoo, in Providence, in nothing.

Naturally, culturally, everyone is superstitious to some

Jerome Herman "Dizzy" Dean warming up for the Chicago Cubs prior to a 1939 game. *(Wide World)*

37

extent or other. Modern cultures, like ours, preserve a good bit of belief and custom left over from discarded, "pagan," religions. Such superstition is not completely ignored. Sometimes it is even modernized and given Christian symbolism. The fact that the number 13 is unlucky or that walking under a ladder is risky are beliefs that go well back before the Last Supper or the idea of the Trinity. Nevertheless, because there were said to be thirteen guests at the supper which Judas shared with Christ and because walking through the triangle formed by the ladder and the wall violates the Trinity, we never bother to think why the early Indo-Europeans, Norse, Greeks, Romans found 13 unlucky or why similar head taboos exist all across the world.

Furthermore, every ballplayer knows three types of superstitions: those beliefs that he brings with him from his main culture; the long-standing superstitions of the game; and his personal superstitions or eccentricities. Frequently, when one reads a collection of baseball superstitions, he discovers most of the contents have little to do with baseball as such. The fact that a fan releases a black cat in front of the Cubs' dugout before a crucial game with the Mets doesn't make a baseball superstition out of "black cats bring bad luck." Nor does the fact that a player may carry a four-leaf clover or a rabbit's foot in his pocket connect those talismans with the game. Typical is the M.A. thesis on *Superstitions of Grayson County* (Kentucky) done at what was then Western Kentucky State College by Eliza A. Fentriss. It has a section entitled "Baseball Beliefs and Customs." Under that heading are such widespread superstitions as these,

Place a piece of black cloth in the dugout of the opposing team, and it will bring good luck to your team.

Outfield great Ty Cobb goes after a high fly for the Detroit Tigers, 1923. *(Wide World)*

If a baseball player sees a cross-eyed woman in the grandstand, he will not get a hit during the game.

It is good luck to pass a wagon loaded with hay as you go to a baseball game.

The black cloth is similar to the black cat, calling up the color symbolic of the Devil; and cross-eyed women are bad luck in all British-derived cultures. The hay wagon is lucky in Wales, lucky in England if you remember to make a wish and spit upon seeing it. John McGraw used this one in the form of a beer wagon with empty barrels to inspire the Giants against the Cubs years ago. After a four-game sweep, presaged by the appearance of the wagon with empty barrels before each game, the players were accosted by a man looking for the manager. He wanted his money for driving the wagon past the ballpark for four straight days "just the way McGraw told him to."

Because backgrounds differ, superstitions of this sort may be a source of embarrassment to the players. Chico Salmon, a Panamanian utility player, was the subject of a rather wry feature in *The Sporting News* of April 26, 1969, because of his fear of ghosts. The tone of the article was superior, implying that Salmon's beliefs were clearly outdated. In fact, he seemed to feel this way himself, and indicated that the intolerance shown his fear of the dark in the U.S. Army did a lot to cure him of his foolishness. The same tone is present in the following account of a standard Caribbean (and American) hex related in *Sports Illustrated* on February 3, 1969:

. . . And Second Baseman Julio Gotay is a fine hitter but bedeviled by the specter of evil spirits. Robinson had to stop one game and race out to see why Gotay would not go near second. Gotay pointed at two crossed sticks that were spooking him. Later, when Robinson was bounced out of the game, Gotay blamed the voodoo rather than the umpire.

Of course, most of the true baseball superstitions depend to some degree or other on more widely held beliefs. Perhaps the idea that the team leading the league on July 4 will win the pennant is unique to baseball, but the seventh-inning stretch is clearly associated with the lucky number 7 of Hebraic-Christian tradition and the habit of yelling "Look out for the dog!" or "Look out for the wheelbarrow!" to protect the infielder who is drifting back on a pop fly is but a variation on similar pointless warnings used by sailors, lumbermen, and hunters. The fact that it is unlucky to leave two bats crossed in front of the dugout is, *Sports Illustrated* to the contrary, cut from pretty much the same cloth as the fear of two crossed sticks that "bedeviled" Julio Gotay. And Leo Durocher's refusal to change his suit all through the 1951 pennant drive of the New York Giants is not unlike the refusal of college students, actors, and other persons facing crises to wear their "lucky ties" or "lucky sweaters." Bob Friend's wife wore the same dress to the ballpark as long as Bob was winning, and Nancy Seaver carried a lucky ring and three or four other lucky objects to assist Tom defeat the Orioles in the 1969 Series. Perhaps Leo carried things a bit farther than most. He bragged, "I'm wearing the same socks, shirt, and underwear, too!"

Naturally, a great many of the superstitions encountered at the ballpark are highly personal: Frank Howard touching second as he trots in from the outfield; Leo Durocher busily picking up all the scraps of paper in the dugout; Pete Rose "hustling" everywhere he goes. Some of these customs are bizarre. Trainer Andy Lotshaw of the old Cubs had to rub Guy Bush's arm with a secret ointment, actually Coca-Cola, before each pitching assignment. One high school coach, eventually named the Twitch Witch, had to remove himself from the lines because his habit of touching his cap and trousers in a superstitious routine confused the baserunners trying to read his signs. Sometimes an idiosyncrasy appeals to others in the group, spreads, eventually becoming one of the general beliefs associated with the game. Perhaps the idea that it is bad luck to change bats after the second strike was once a personal superstition. The idea that it is disastrous to speak of a no-hitter probably began in some individual misfortune.

This latter superstition is a very famous one, often as honored in the breach as it is in the observance. It is interesting to read the remarks published in the Los Angeles *Times* of July 6, 1962, concerning a no-hitter Sandy Koufax threw at the Mets.

When Sandy Koufax of the Los Angeles Dodgers pitched a no-hit game, June 30, 1962, against the New York Mets, he was interviewed on this point after the game, and admitted that none of his teammates had mentioned the fact. He said, however, that he knew "he had one going." Solly Hemus, Met coach, broke the tabu by referring to it in the late innings, as follows: "Do you still have it?" and then finally started to say, "Let's break up this no-hitter." Koufax admitted that in the last inning his catcher, Roseboro, called the pitches from the point of view of the "no-hitter," rather than from considerations of general strategy. Koufax summed up by saying, "You're either going to do it, or you're not. It's not what someone says, but what you do on the field." From the fourth inning on in this same game, the Dodger announcers, Vin Scully and Jerry Doggett, kept making reference to the fact that Koufax had a no-hit game in prospect. In an interview with Scully, sports columnist Sid Ziff quoted Scully as being amazed at not receiving a single telegram protesting his jinxing the pitcher by mentioning the pitching feat. This had apparently happened in the four or five other no-hitters he had defied tradition by reporting over the years.

Like superstitions, proverbs are a way in which people transfer behavior patterns, ethics, and standards from one generation to the next. "The wit of one, the wisdom of many" they have been described, and human beings never tire of using them once they have found them. Proverbs ("The trades you don't make are your best ones") are related to a number of similar forms such as the aphorism or maxim (Grantland Rice's "It's not whether you win or lose, but how you play the game"); the truism ("Southpaws are wild"); the Wellerism ("Meet you at home, as one baseline said to the other"); the slogan ("All the way with LA"); the conventional phrase ("Kill the umpire"); the popular comparison ("Wild as a hawk")—and to separate one from the other can be difficult indeed. My feeling is that a phrase can be considered proverbial when it possesses two elements: when it has become an anonymous statement of practical knowledge for a group; when its language shows signs of being metaphorical or inevitable: that is, poetic. Mike Gonzalez' "Good field, no hit" is a conventional phrase, for it is not a statement of group wisdom. Ring Lardner's "He can't field, but he sure can't hit" is an aphorism, for it is still considered Lardner's, not the group's. "Throw curves to batters you have never seen before" is a truism, because it lacks poetry. But "Don't pitch a country boy high" is a proverb. At any rate, one thing is certain: when you can distinguish the proverbs of a people you know the people and know them well.

Most of the proverbial and near-proverbial lore of the ballplayers never leaves the confines of the ballpark. However, a few phrases have become well-known. Certainly the most famous is the cynical statement "Nice guys finish last," now definitively attributed to Leo Durocher and included in the latest editions of *Bartlett's Familiar Quotations.* Durocher himself has never really claimed the phrase which he is said to have coined in the mid-1940s. According to Leo's story he was sitting on the bench as manager of the Brooklyn Dodgers before a game with the New York Giants. Seeing opposing manager Mel Ott, he claims to have remarked something of this sort to a group of writers which included Frank Graham: "Yeah, look at Ott. He's such a nice guy and they'll finish last for him." Then seeing Sid Gordon, Buddy Kerr, Bobby Thomson, and Walker Cooper together on the bench, he continued, "All nice guys, and they'll finish last." Credit for the inevitable phrasing, "the wit of one," probably belongs to one of the writers who heard the comment. Yet no one has stepped forth to claim it, so Leo might as well relax and enjoy himself. Like all aphorisms that become proverbial, this one is now the property of the English-speaking people, and it matters no more who originated it than who originated "Don't cross your bridges until you come to them." To repeat, this is the main distinction between a proverb and an aphorism. As long as credit for the wit and wisdom belongs to a specific individual, the phrase is an aphorism. Once the phrase becomes the practical knowledge belonging to a group or a culture, then it is a proverb. "Nice guys finish last" has moved into the realm of proverb. People who know nothing of baseball use it. Leo's other phrase, "I'd trip my mother as she rounded third if it meant saving a run" has remained an aphorism, the broader culture, as yet, unwilling to accept the wisdom of such an action.

Another aphorism which has become proverbial for American sports officials, if not for the public at large, is Umpire Bill Klem's "I never missed one in my heart." So seriously did Klem take this statement of umpiring integrity that he claimed to have retired in 1941, the first time he ever wondered if he had called a play correctly—a tag at second on an attempted steal. Other aphorisms that have

Michael "King" Kelly, base-stealer extraordinaire prior to the turn of the century. *(Culver Pictures, Inc.)*

become proverbial in the profession are Willie Keeler's "Hit 'em where they ain't" and some now long-forgotten general manager's "The trades you don't make are your best ones." Satchel Paige's remark, "Don't look back, something might be gaining on you" is a deserving candidate, as is Branch Rickey's remark that Leo Durocher had the ability of "taking a bad situation and making it immediately worse."

While the bulk of the proverbial matter in the game is too parochial for general use, one mustn't underestimate its role in the occupation. Johnny Vandermeer, standing on the mound in June of 1938; facing the inevitable Leo Durocher with two out, the bases full, and the count 2 and 2; on the brink of being the first man in the history of the majors to pitch back-to-back no-hitters, turned to an occupational proverb to help himself psychologically. "Go to Powder River," he told himself. In translation, if you are going to fail on the brink of a remarkable accomplishment, fail with your best. Don't throw something you'll regret. So Vandermeer threw a fastball, Durocher flied to center, and he came through, saved "in the day when heaven was falling" by the wisdom of many who had learned over the years to "Go to Powder River" (the best in Western equipment).

Much of the group wisdom has never been phrased well enough to be called proverbial and remains at the level of truism. All pitchers know the general principle, "Never throw a weak hitter a change-up." This is almost a proverb, but it lacks poetry. And the idea that you keep your fastball up and your curve down has never been inevitably phrased. But truisms can be quite specific. It was common knowledge around the American League fifty or sixty years ago that you did nothing to stir up Ty Cobb. "Don't get him mad" or "Let him sleep" were ideas stressed before playing the Tigers. The phrases served as near-proverbs when Cobb was around. They are so applicable to certain athletes that they are dragged out again and again, for Walter Johnson, for Jackie Robinson, for Richie Allen, for basketball star Wilt Chamberlain.

Between the proverb, aphorism, and truism and the area of folk speech lies a region in which dwell the slogan, the popular comparison, and the conventional phrase. Baseball has given birth to a great many slogans, most coined by writers and publicity men. The majority are ephemeral, dying with pennant hopes in October. From the Gaelic call-to-arms, *slaugh gairm*, these verbal flags are essential to situations where "the troops" need something to rally

around. Usually serving a specific moment, they seldom become proverbial. "First in war, first in peace, first in the hearts of his countrymen" can be used for persons other than George Washington by people speaking colloquial American, but something like "First in shoes, first in booze, last in the American League" (of St. Louis industries and the Browns) has very limited application. The chances of that slogan's becoming deeply imbedded in the language or spreading beyond the game are as poor as those of "Go, go, Chicago." Perhaps the two most famous baseball slogans are "From Tinker to Evers to Chance," a phrase created in a Franklin Adams poem to immortalize the double-play combination of the old Cubs: Joe Tinker, Johnny Evers, and Frank Chance; and "Slide, Kelly, Slide," the phrase made famous by followers of jaunty "King Kell." Others that have enjoyed some currency are substitute J. C. "Blondy" Ryan's famous telegram to the 1934 Giants whom he was rejoining after being injured: "We can't lose now. Am en route"; Bill Terry's unfortunate remark of the winter of 1934, "Is Brooklyn still in the National League?", a question which became the Dodgers' battle cry during the following season; and the Boston Braves' "Spahn, Sain, and two days of rain" as those two pitchers carried the load in the late stages of the 1948 pennant drive.

Slogans are very close to conventional phrases, which are frequently memorable comments that have become anonymous. Tim Hurst's "You can't beat the hours," a phrase by which he rationalized the low-paying profession of the umpire in the days before night ball, or the wistful "Wait till next year" are good examples. So is the phrasing derived from the last lines of Ernest Thayer's poem, "Casey at the Bat": "there is no joy in Mudville" or "the mighty Casey has struck out." A lawyer loses a casual tennis match against a pal; shaking hands with his opponent, he remarks, "Just wait till next year." A broker picks up the paper on the way to work and reads that the Cubs have blown a crucial series to the Mets, commenting, "There's no joy in Mudville today." A teacher remarks about his low salary, adding, "Yeah, but you can't beat the hours."

Sometimes it is hard to distinguish between such phrases and popular comparisons, excepting that the latter are metaphorical. "Loose as a goose" is a popular comparison derived from baseball. This phrase has changed meaning since it began, no later than the 1930s. Originally, the phrase was "Loose as a goose and twice as shifty," referring to a clumsy ballplayer As it was shortened to its present form, it began to be used to describe indifference to pressure. From it has come the conventionalized phrase "loosey goosey" as used by Willie Mays to describe the San Francisco Giants in the last of the ninth as they were defeating the Dodgers in the final game of the 1962 playoff: "We was all loosey-goosey out there!" Such things are so close to the realm of folk speech, I think I had better turn to that subject at once.

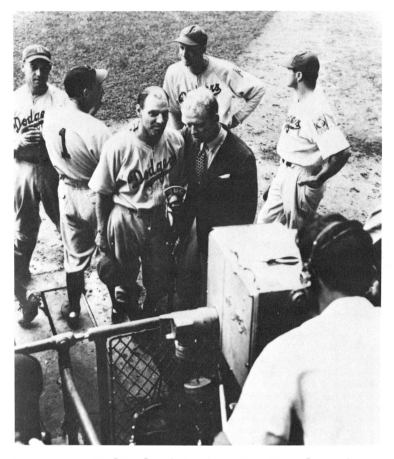

Sportscaster Red Barber interviews Leo Durocher prior to the first telecast of a major league baseball game on August 26, 1939 at Ebbets Field. In background are (left to right): Cincinnati Reds manager Deacon Bill McKechnie (No. 1), Dodgers' Dolph Camilli and Dixie Walker. *(Wide World)*

New York Mets manager Yogi Berra gives "thumbs up" sign
after his team defeated Oakland, 10–7,
to even up the 1973 World Series at one game apiece.
Relief pitcher Tug McGraw (center) embraces Berra
and Mets first baseman Willie Mays. (Wide World)

BASEBALL TALK

I AM not at all certain, even after 25 years of using the term, that there is anything that can be clearly defined as folk speech. Supposedly, folk speech is the dialect used by a particular folk group, an idea that is simple enough until one realizes that language habits are very persistent habits. Thus, a man's folk speech may survive long after he has become highly educated, or at least long after he has embraced the mainstream written culture of his nation. Certainly there is no such thing as the folk speech of baseball players, for ball players come from many different backgrounds, speaking many different ways. They are not together long enough to develop their own dialect. What they do develop is a cant or special vocabulary that is characteristic of their trade. The White hillbilly, the city Italian, the southern Black, the Cuban, the Mexican, all learn this cant and share it, but they continue to communicate in the particular dialect or type of speech they grew up with and use at home. However, the cant of ballplayers is not something that can be dismissed lightly. As baseball has flourished, this specialized language has infiltrated the English we Americans use, contributing colorfully at almost every level.

A simple way of dividing our language levels is in three: vulgar, standard, formal or literary. Vulgar language is the language of the uneducated and semi-educated. It is full of what educated people call "grammatical inaccuracies" and archaic bits of usage. A phrase like "I ain't takin' nuthin' from nobody" is characteristic. Rural dialects and the speech of most folk groups fall into this category. Standard English is the language by which the business of the country is carried on. This is the language of ordinary, schooled merchants, professional men, and polite people. Formal or literary English is the language which one finds in serious books, which is used in formal speaking situations, and which is carefully combed for grammatical "errors" and bits of "inferior" speech. These categories overlap to a degree. Both vulgar and standard English, for example, are filled with slang, which is a highly ephemeral, fashionable, usually colorful means of quite informal day-to-day communication. Slang is always feeding words and phrases into standard English, some of which become so firmly entrenched that they are even acceptable in formal English. Polite, but informal, standard English may be described as colloquial—a speech which is not incorrect or vulgar, but which is rather more slangy than standard normally is. Language areas do shift, if rather slowly, as time passes, and sometimes the colloquial speech of yesterday is the formal speech of today. What's more, all speakers move back and forth from one area of speech to another as situations change. Of course, it is easier to shift down than up, and a user of vulgar English is seldom successful in trying to move up to formal, or even colloquial-standard speech.

We are interested in a special cant: that of baseball. This cant, when used exclusively, is nearly unintelligible to an outsider. However, much of it has entered slang and colloquial speech, a good bit has thus become acceptable in the most conservative standard speech, and a little in

First base umpire Ron Luciano puts his all into "yeer out" (left) and "Saaafe!" (right) signals. (Wide World)

formal American English. The overall contribution of this cant is truly amazing. No other sport has contributed even a fraction of the phrases and words baseball has. There is some truth in the statement that a foreigner wishing to learn our language might as well start in the ballpark.

For even the most inattentive of Americans know perfectly well the meaning of words and phrases such as "benchwarmer," "rooter," "bleachers," "beanball," "southpaw," "pop up," or "pinch-hitter." Sometimes verbs formed from these words are also widely used. "To pinch hit" is what grammarians call a back-formation from the noun "pinch-hitter," a substitute for the regular batter. In baseball, a pinch-hitter is usually a better, or at least a more suitable, hitter than the man he replaces. However, as the noun and verb have moved into colloquial, then into standard, and now even into formal speech, the meaning has shifted slightly. In non-baseball situations, "to pinch hit" means simply to substitute for someone, usually with the implication that an emergency exists. The pinch-hitter is not likely to be of the same ability as the person being replaced. Other words and conventional phrases that most Americans are at ease with are "grandstand catch," with its associated verb "to grandstand"; "doubleheader"; "hot stove league"; "to strike out" or even "to fan"; "to have two strikes on you"; "shut out"; "on the bench"; "in there pitching"; "to get one's innings"; "to be caught off base"; "to have something on the ball," "to be out in left field"; "that was a real curveball"; "to warm up"; "to be farmed out"; "out of my league." There are a lot more. Some of them, like the phrase "to get to first base," have been extended in strange ways. In colloquial or standard English when one says, "I never got to first base," he means that he

Baseball announcer Walter "Red" Barber broadcasting from the radio booth at Ebbets Field in 1943. *(Wide World)*

has failed completely—or in other baseball parlance, "Struck out." However, in teen-age slang of pre-World War II days, the whole diamond was used to indicate the sexual progress a boy might make with a girl. Here "getting to first base" indicated kissing the girl; each additional base represented a further liberty, progressing toward the ultimate "home run." Many of the words and phrases listed above have moved so far away from their cant beginnings that people use them without thinking where they come from. Slowly, but surely, they are integrating themselves into the English spoken carefully by the best-educated Americans.

Nonetheless, words can remain at the colloquial or slang level for long, long periods of time, no longer just cant, yet not moving into the best speech. The word "phoney" is an extremely old bit of underworld cant which is still marked slang in most dictionaries. A word such as "southpaw" to designate a left hander may never become standard American English, but it is unlikely it will vanish from slang usage, where it is presently lodged. "Bush league" is similar. "Bush league" is rapidly becoming more and more acceptable in American speech. It may never enter formal American English, perhaps never enter standard. But it is no longer a cant term. A football or basketball player, even a man in business, may be referred to as "bush league," although there are really no "bush" leagues in football, basketball, or business. Furthermore, "bush league" has been shortened to "bush," which has become a handy synonym for cheap, for childish, for inexperienced.

Baseball cant itself is of two sorts. The specialized language that the average fan understands, even though his less involved wife or daughter may not, and the language that only the hardcore players, coaches, writers, and front office men know. The first sort of cant, what we might call "slang-cant" to show that a good many persons outside the occupation know and use it, involves such terms as "toe the slab" (prepare to pitch), "hook" (curve), "duster" (pitch thrown at the batter), "taking" (letting a pitch go by without swinging), "automatic strike" (a pitch thrown when everyone knows the batter will be taking), "Texas Leaguer" (short outfield fly), "Baltimore chop" (ball that hits in front of the plate and bounces high), "jam" (throw an in-

side pitch), and the like. Anyone who follows the game in the most casual of ways, anyone who has played the game, knows this language. However, many a person who will recognize what is meant by a curve, a strike, a fly; who will recognize the name Willie Mays, but not Willie McCovey; who watches the World Series but no other games will draw a blank if confronted by this sort of slang-cant.

On the other hand, there are a great many people who are lifelong ball fans who never learn the hardcore cant of the game. Phrases such as "a cup of coffee" (a brief stay in the majors); "low bridge" (knock a batter down); "downtown one" (hit a homer); "mustard" (speed on a fast ball); "really bringing it" (throwing hard); "wearing the horns" (to be the goat); "hang a clothesline" (hit a line drive); "unbutton your shirt" (swing hard); "wheelhouse" (area of one's hitting strength); "ground hog" (groundskeeper); "Murphy money" (the spending money given in spring training); "cripple" (a pitch which has to be over) are seldom used beyond the ballpark. Sometimes such expressions are more widely recognized in one grammatical form than in another. The word "hanging" in "a hanging curve" would be known to more people than the verb "to hang one," which has developed from it. The same would be true of "to take a pitch" and "to take one."

Like all cant, baseball cant comes and goes with amazing rapidity. There aren't many ballplayers or sportswriters today who could tell you what "a fizzle" or "a plugger" is, even though they would recognize the more modern equivalents "a skull" (a dumb play) or "a rooter"; what "hit the bumps" means, though they would recognize "a slugfest"; what an "à la carte" catch is, though they would recognize "circus catch" (a spectacular catch). Moreover,

**Willie Mays protests call on a close play
during his San Francisco Giants days.
Coach Whitey Lockman puts in his two cents' worth,
but umpire Jocko Conlan remains unmoved.** *(Wide World)*

JUDGMENT! JUDGMENT!
HOW THE UMPIRE MAY YET BE COMPELLED TO DEFEND HIMSELF.

An 1888 cartoon suggests "how the umpire may be compelled to defend himself." *(New York Public Library)*

some of the cant has shifted its meaning as words are wont to do. Ask a ballplayer today what "a hard one" is and he will tell you a fastball. Not too long ago "a hard one" meant the first pitch thrown to a batter; usually it was a fastball. Ask a ballplayer what a "chucker" is and he will tell you a pitcher. Once "chucker" meant a pitcher with nothing but a fastball, no curve or change-up. Few ballplayers refer to a weak fly, "a Texas Leaguer," as "a banjo" or "a Japanese liner" anymore, but they still use the phrase "banjo hitter" (a weak hitter). Nor do they call the ballpark "the garden" or "the orchard," though they still refer to the outfield as the "outer garden" or the "outer orchard." With so many Latins in today's line-ups, a lot of people have forgotten that "a Cuban" was an American Negro in the days before the color line had been broken. Sometimes even the players themselves are uncertain whether a term is "in" or "out." In the spring of 1969, pitcher Jerry Johnson was interviewed on the radio. He told how he had rid his pitching motion of a little "crow hop" (an extra step at the end) during winter ball. Two weeks later members of the Houston Astros, interviewed for me by Bill Giles, denied the phrase was still in use.

Nothing sounds cornier than out-of-date cant. To hear someone refer to the "truck-horse" of the staff or to a player who has "frozen" a liner embarrasses everyone within hearing distance, even though we are perfectly happy to hear about the "workhorse" or the "bellwether" of the staff or about a player who has "speared" or "gobbled up" a liner. This is something that bothers modern readers of "Casey at the Bat" where Flynn is referred to as a "pudding" and Blake as a "fake" and where the fans yell "fraud" at the umpire, although we don't mind Flynn's

Plate umpire Paul Runge signals "Safe" after jubilant Pittsburgh Pirates second baseman Rennie Stennett (left) scored the winning run against the Mets. Catcher Duffy Dyer sprawls at right. *(Wide World)*

"a-hugging" third, the fans hoping Casey might get "a whack at that," or the fact the ball is called a "sphere." This is because the proper use of cant indicates belonging, distinguishes the "ins" from the "outs"—and one must have his cant up-to-date or run the risk of being labelled an "out." *The Sporting News*, known in the cant of the trade as "the Bible," enjoys stressing the "in" nature of its readers by using large amounts of "in-language" in the headlines, although the stories themselves, many of which are reprinted from newspapers with broader readerships, are in colloquial standard American and use only a minimum of slang-cant. Such phrases as TRIBE FLYHAWKS CARRY BIG WARCLUBS or PETE'S REPEATER PISTOL OFF TO RED-HOT START are headlines from that publication. Only one who has followed the game avidly could translate the information that the outfielders of the Cleveland Indians are heavy hitters or that "Pistol Pete" Rose of the Cincinnati Reds has been hitting consistently in spring training. In fifty years, perhaps no one but a specialist will be able to translate it at all.

It is most revealing to look over H. L. Mencken's list of baseball terms published but a generation or so ago. Surely there are plenty of terms still current on that list: "snake," "strawberry," "duster," "wolves," "rooter," "rubber," "glass arm," "hot corner"; but there are already a number that make us think we are looking through a glass at some now-vanished world: "county fair" (show off); "pool-table" (smooth infield); "pay-station" (home plate); "pillow" (base); "mackerel" (curve). Each was the product of some colorful or imaginative player, coach, announcer, or writer who associated himself with the game, lending it his localisms or his creations as the case might be. So quickly so many of them have died, forgotten as the originator moved on to other tasks. I recall one ballplayer who referred to flyballs as "bears." He said he was going out there in the field to "shoot those bears," meaning he was going to catch everything that came near him. Pretty soon all members of the team called flies "bears" and the phrase became part of our local baseball cant. But the phrase never spread. It died in the 1930s, remembered now as a bit of *auld lang syne* by a handful of people. George Scott's habit of referring to home runs as "taters" or "them long taters" will probably die when he is given his final release. On the other hand, Red Barber's "sitting in the catbird seat" was pretty widely known for awhile—widely enough known that James Thurber was willing to use it as a title for one of his stories. But the phrase, which means to be in control of the situation, is clearly not going to live. When I teach the Thurber story to college students today, they have to ask what the phrase means. However, the expression "charley horse," referring to a mildly pulled leg muscle, became part of the cant of ballplayers, slowly spread to colloquial slang, to standard American English, and now is so deeply embedded in our language that most people would have trouble describing the ailment if the phrase were taken from them. In fact, the *Journal of the Medical Association* printed an article as long ago as November 30, 1946, entitled "Treatment of the Charley Horse," rather than "Treatment of Injury to Quadriceps Femoris." Such a usage indicates the phrase to have been a part of even the most formal American English for a quarter of a century.

Cant, like all language, has some amazing inconsistencies within it. Phrases like "hit the dirt," "homer," or "chased" have to be placed in context for meaning. "Hit the dirt" can refer to being "low-bridged" (thrown at) or it can refer to sliding, especially on a throw from the outfield. A "homer" may be a four-base smash, a "circuit clout," but it can also mean an umpire who favors the home team. And an umpire called "a homer" is likely to "chase" the player involved, even though a pitcher can also get "chased" by the batters who knock him out of the box. A fielder can "boot" a flyball, even though the verb originates in someone's appearing to "kick" a grounder instead of fielding it cleanly. A pitcher can remark that he "used to be a thrower" but has now "become a pitcher." His friends will know that he refers to the fact that he has learned to rely on savvy, change of speeds, and hitting the corners rather that simply "throwing hard" all the time. Silly as the following conversation sounds, it makes perfectly good sense to anyone knowledgeable in baseball cant.

"How are ya' hittin' 'em?"

"Real good now. Last year I was just a swinger, but now I've learned to hit."

"What's the difference?"

"This year I'm relaxed. I go up there and swing. I'm no longer trying to hit every pitch out of here."

Furthermore, there is nothing to prevent the "sparkplug of the well-oiled machine" from "gobbling up" "a clothesline" or a "blue darter," or to prevent the "bellwether" of the "flippers" from being the "workhorse" of the staff. Obviously, such words as "sparkplug," "bellwether," and "blue darter" have been around so long that no one thinks of them as metaphors. No one thinks of the term "gopher ball" metaphorically either. A "gopher ball" (a pitch that is easy to hit) has nothing to do with rodents. It is merely a pitch that the batter will "go for"—a folk etymology that has developed much in the way "Welsh rabbit" has developed from "Welsh rarebit" or "sparrow grass" has developed from "asparagus."

The use of prepositions in this sort of language is as whimsical as it is in the rest of English. For instance, a batter can go down to first on a walk; he can then go down or over to second; but he will not go down to third. He will go over there, and come in to home plate. He goes up to the plate to bat, but will go back, not down, to the dugout, although the phrase "one down" or "two down" lets you know how many have come up unsuccessfully. Perhaps there is some geometric logic in all this, but there is none in the verb "to loosen up," derived from the more sensible "to tighten up." Yet language is always this way, and one learns to speak it properly or he finds himself "out."

How vital a cant can be is demonstrated quite clearly by looking at baseball terms in Spanish. *Beisbol* has become a particularly popular game in the Latin American countries. The game is played exactly as it is in the States, and many of the better Latin professionals spend their summers in our majors and minors. Baseball terms, along with the rules and the equipment, have long since gone "south of the border"—often with no change. Words like "base," "hit," "error," "infield," "put out," and "shortstop" have simply entered Latin American speech and have, at least as far as baseball goes, become as genuinely Spanish as "kindergarten" or "gauche" are English. Some like "*doble header*" (doubleheader) or "*ládron de bases*" (basestealer) are partially translated; others like "*receptor*" (catcher), "*juego de estrellas*" (all-star game),

"*cubrir terreno*" (cover ground), and "*llevar la delantera*" (to take the lead) are literally translated; others like "*curva*" (curve), "*batear*" (to bat) or "*batear por*" (to bat for) are simply hispanicized English. Most interesting are those cant phrases that cross the language barrier literally. Thus to shut out a team is (to) "*blanquear*" (blank or whitewash) them, "*un jardinero*" (a gardener) is an outfielder, to score a run is (to) "*cruzar la goma*" (to cross the rubber, the plate). Whitewash and gardener are cant words, not always understood by non-baseball-oriented Americans; rubber for plate is also cant, but not a term used frequently in the States. "*Goma*" shows that new bits of cant are beginning to creep into Spanish baseball talk. A fly ball, often referred to as a "*palomita*" (a little dove) by Latins, is never called that in the States, although appropriately Americans call an outfielder a "flyhawk."

One finds exact parallels in the Canadian French of Montreal where the newspapers are now filled with such terms as "*faux ballon*" (foul ball), "*lanceur de relève*" (relief pitcher), "*au jeu*" (play ball), "*mitaine de receveur*" (catcher's mitt), "*erreur*" (error), and "*circuit*" (home run, "circuit smash"). It is similar in Japan. Of course, as baseball survives in these lands, fresh cant must develop; but particularly in Latin American and Canada where the ties to the States are extremely close, the changes will be slow in coming.

I suspect the sportswriters and the announcers have been more influential in the development of baseball's special language than the players themselves. Facing the tedious task of describing the same events day after day, the newsmen and announcers frequently rely on colorful language to make the routine dramatic. In fact, so standard is this device that a number of announcers like Red Barber and Dizzy Dean have made colorful speech almost an end in itself with their "bases F.O.B." (bases full of Brooklyns) and their "slud" into third. As ballplayers are literate and as they listen to games on the radio before, during, and after the time they are in the occupation, they rely heavily on these often highly ingenious imaginations. So, in an endless cycle, they "whiff," "take the K," "fan" or "hit for the circuit," "the roundtripper," the "grandslam" off "twirlers," "hurlers," "chuckers" who long to "toss goose eggs" at them, "whitewash" them, "corral" them.

Nonetheless, there are plenty of imaginative ballplayers, the Willie Ramsdells, the Rocky Bridges, the Frank Robinsons. Such men, the skilled "bench jockeys" (coaches or players who specialize in "riding" their opponents), serve as a source of much colorful phrasing. A good bench jockey is worth a lot, and players have managed to hang on because of their skill with words well after their skill with bat and glove has faded. Phrases such as "hot dog" (a show-off), "rabbit ears" (a sensitive opponent or umpire), and "choke" (tighten up in crucial situations) have risen out of the shenanigans of the men on the sidelines. In fact, so strong is the feeling concerning the word "choke" that a player needs only to hold his hand to his throat after an umpire's decision to get thrown out of the game.

This brings up the whole subject of ritualized insults within the game: the sort of thing that ghetto Blacks call "sounding" or "signifying." Almost all groups develop patterns of verbal play that enable people to kid each other and the culture in which they live without actually antagonizing anyone or forcing anyone to fight. This sort of interplay always has rules or signals that tell both participants and onlookers that the affair is mock, not real. The rules vary tremendously from time to time, level of society to level of society, and place to place. The meaningful nonsense which the fool of the medieval court was licensed to direct at both courtiers and king was of this sort. The wars of wit that fill seventeenth-century comedy indicating not only *savoir faire* but, when between the sexes, entrance into courtship; the *bon mot* jousts of twentieth-century intellectuals; the fencings of near-catty women are other examples—although in each of these the approved approach is subtle rather than frontal.

At the folk level, ritualized verbal play nearly always takes the simplest and least sophisticated form of wit: the direct insult. Blacks, country Whites, Puerto Ricans, Mexicans, urban boys of all sorts learn appropriate rituals for this purpose; and success in word-play, even at this anti-intellectual level, is an important means of manifesting leadership. For instance, an American Black coming into professional ball has long since been playing the dozens or sounding with youngsters of his own race, running through patterns that start with phrases like "your mother eats garbage" and continue through obscene replies and counter-replies such as "your father eats horse-shit" or "your sister is a railroad track, lays all over the country" or "your girl friend is cake, everyone gets their piece."

Black ballplayers, like Whites or Latins, may while away the time on a bus or plane trip with such interchanges, allowing the "in" language and the familiar patterns to isolate and protect them from the other players. When the process breaks down, and someone takes an insult literally, usually by actually denying it, then trouble ensues and a fight may well begin. I recall an incident reported between an American Black and a Latin Black on the Atlanta Braves a couple of years back. The Latin evidently insulted the American personally with a reference too pungent to be quoted in the papers: I assume one that referred either to incest or to homosexuality. "You Black———!" he is supposed to have said. The American discussing the resultant fisticuffs was heard to remark, "I don't mind him calling me Black. After all, he isn't exactly pink himself, but no one can call me a ——— and get away with it." It is interesting to note that a White player might not have been able to use either word (certainly not in "that" tone of voice), while another American Black might have been able to get by with both words, especially had he flown the proper signal flags first. In brief, as outsiders seldom comprehend the rules of "sounding," it is next to impossible to play this way across racial or linguistic barriers where sensitivities cloud the mock and the real. Consequently, baseball has developed its own insult patterns from within, free of those patterns brought to the dugout and locker room from the varied regional and ethnic cultures.

"Bench jockeying" is one way in which baseball has developed its own sounding. Conventional phrases referring to the umpire's seeing-eye dog, to the batter's inability to hit the ball with a barndoor, to the pitcher's candy arm stand available and pre-packaged. Rules have developed over the years and taboos are well-known. Bill Klem, the most famous of the major-league umpires, used to draw a line on the ground during a rhubarb. If a player stepped over that line he was out of the game. Klem's line is a symbol applicable not only to player-umpire relationships, but to player-fan and player-player relationships as well. For an umpire or another player will take a surprising amount of abuse if the proper clichés are used and the matter doesn't drag on too long. For example, a catcher, commenting on the eyesight of an umpire, might get away with the remark, "What do you do in the off season? Sell pencils on the sidewalk?" providing he did not turn around or indicate to the fans and benches that he was trying to show the umpire up. But were he to make the same remark while turning to the umpire or while "jawing" with him or to shout it and related clichés from the bench too persistently, he would probably be "sent to the showers." Of course, human factors have a lot to do with such matters. Every umpire, every player differs. Schoolboy Rowe was ridden by the national press as well as by the bench jockeys for his naïve remark, "How'm I doin', Edna?" made to his fiancée during a 1934 radio interview. He took it pretty well. But Bill Klem was willing to give anyone the thumb under any conditions for calling him "Catfish." It seemed, when he was working in the American Association he had called a play against the Columbus club then managed by Bill Clymer. Clymer challenged Klem, who turned away, trying not to pay attention. "Why you old, you old, you old . . . catfish!" Clymer shouted at him, "You can't talk, you can't smile, you can't do anything but move your gills!" "Catfish," picked up by the bench jockeys,

Oakland Athletics' Joe Rudi slaps hands with teammates who crowd out of dugout to congratulate him after he drove a home run to left field in the second game of the 1972 World Series. *(Wide World)*

became a personal, vicious insult in Klem's book and moved bench jockeying from sounding into the realm of invective. Thus, ballplayers seldom tire of anecdotes about players who have overstepped the "line" and gotten away with it: asking some umpire how he got his square head in the round mask, remarking, "If you call them any lower

I'll get a niblick instead of a bat," explaining "If you look through the open spaces in the mask you'll improve your calls," and so forth.

Nowhere is the distinction between ritualized and personal insult any clearer than it is in American Black-White relationships. Any White can mock a Black catcher with a conventionalized phrase such as "Another bad call, man! —How can you mothers win with that stonehead behind the plate?"—even if the remark is sprinkled with obscenity; but a reference to skin-color, to poverty, to background: for instance, "Another bad call, boy!" may bring retaliation not only from the opponent, but also from members of the White's own team. This is one of the things that all Black ballplayers resented most in the days when the color-line was being broken. Then so much of the bench-jockeying directed at the obviously self-conscious Black players was not ritualized and, especially in the case of Southern players, represented deep-seated social attitudes.

Nor should one forget that the jeers and yells of the fans are loosely controlled in the same fashion. Much of the early resentment in Boston against Ted Williams was that he took ritualized booing and jeering personally. Consequently, as soon as it was obvious that this "rabbit-eared" leftfielder would not play the player-fan game according to the conventions, the conventions were dropped and matters got out of hand. There are fine lines, but they are drawn. And the participants do a pretty good job of learning them. For when the rules are observed, ritualized insult becomes a strong perpetuator of homogeneity. Just knowing what one can and can't get away with binds one to a profession in a way few other ties can.

Equally ritualized is the use of sign language. Like all sports before huge, yelling throngs, baseball has developed a group of hand and body signals, many of which have moved beyond the game into everyday usage. The palms down sign for "safe" is known all over America, not only to indicate that a tennis shot is good, but also to indicate that there is no real problem in a particular situation. The raised thumb for "out" with the associated phrase "to get the thumb" (be thrown out of the game) is also common, as is the sign for "choking" mentioned a few pages back. The habit that players have of slapping each others' palms after a good play or homer has really spread. This began with the insouciance of sluggers who self-consciously preferred to slap an upturned palm rather than shake hands with the on-deck hitter after "such a routine matter" as a four-bagger. It has caught on in basketball, track, soccer, and football and is now pretty well the accepted means of athletic congratulation. Nor can we forget that many such signs have ritualized speech to go with them. The elaborate "steeeerike" call of the umpire accompanies his individual body gyrations; the ritualized "yeeeer out" goes with the raised thumb.

There is also a series of signs used to communicate from bench to field and from position to position. Thus, the catcher tells the pitcher what to throw, the manager tells the bullpen to warm up the southpaw, the first-base umpire tells the plate umpire if the batter has broken his wrists, the batter tells the baserunner that he is putting on the hit-and-run. In fact, so routine are most of the signs that sometimes players will go against the basic ritual of the game to trick one another. Normally, if a man is stealing second and the batter fouls the pitch, either the umpire or the man taking the throw will put his hands up to tell the runner the ball is dead and that he need not slide, possibly hurting himself. If a shortstop were to give this information falsely and then tag the runner because he had failed to slide, the shortstop is liable for retaliation for breaking a basic trust of the game. He may get dusted the next time at bat, he may get the relay of a double-play ball in the teeth, or he may get spiked. If he does, even his own team-mates will understand why.

There are a lot of anecdotes about the signs that coaches give to indicate when the hit-and-run, bunt, or steal is on. The most famous is the one usually told about Charlie Dressen at a now half-forgotten All-Star game. Supposedly the All-Stars were together before the game attempting to come up with a series of signals for the day. Dressen, who was a noted sign-stealer, is thought to have said, "Forget it, I'll give each of you the ones used on your own team." Actually, that is not so far-fetched. There is an amazing traditionalism in sign-giving. The third-base coach almost invariably relays the manager's signals to the players. Even the signs themselves which involve some pattern of touching cap, skin, shirt, belt, pants are firmly entrenched. In fact, a good coach on the opposing club is often better at reading them than a thick player who supposedly knows the pat-tern. A famous ox-like fellow, such as Zeke Bonura of the old White Sox, often ends up as the hero of such stories. The third-base coach puts on the bunt sign, the batter fails to read it. He puts it on again and again. Finally, the opposing manager walks out, taps the batter on the shoulder, and tells him he is meant to bunt, perhaps adding that the pitch will be high and hard. However, as every-one who has ever followed baseball knows when the sacri-fice is going to be used and as all ballplayers know the

pitcher is likely to keep the ball high and hard in that situation, the transmittal of information is more ritual than anything else. But routine though they be, signs are as much a part of baseball as bidding is of bridge, and one does have to remember that they serve functions some-times overlooked. For instance, it helps a catcher tre-mendously to know what sort of pitch is coming, and there is real physical risk if he does not. Often he is signalling for his own safety and efficiency as much as for anything else. Just watch him rush out to the mound if his pitcher crosses him up.

A good sign stealer can always get a job. Men like Charlie Dressen, Casey Stengel, Del Baker, Art Fletcher, Frank Crosetti, Lefty O'Doul, Bob Turley, and Gil Hodges have won dozens of major league games through this skill alone, and ballplayers never tire of yarns about espionage and counter-espionage, like the one that tells how New York Yankee Billy Martin intercepted Brooklyn Dodger manager Charlie Dressen's signal for a squeeze bunt in the 1953 World Series because Dressen carelessly used the same sign he had used when managing Martin in the Pacific Coast League a few years before, or the one that tells how Hank Greenberg nearly had his head torn off because Del Baker signalled him that a curve was coming just before the pitcher threw a high, inside fastball. There is also a pattern of belief and anecdote centering about other tricks to gain an unfair advantage, watering the basepaths or sloping the foul lines when a bunt and steal team comes to town, freezing baseballs to help a weak hitting, good fielding club. Supposedly the first profes-sional in this whole business was Dan Murphy, who worked for the Philadelphia Athletics in the early part of the century. Murphy stationed himself on a roof-top beyond the centerfield wall and with the help of binoculars and a weathervane tipped the batters off to the signals the catcher right behind them was giving to the pitcher. Inevitably, Murphy got into the following trouble: one day the wind blew so hard and erratically he couldn't control the vane and the batters, continually crossed up, nearly got killed. Murphy's trick recurs from time to time with scoreboard operators, second basemen, baserunners doing the same thing. There is, it seems, a moral code here—when a uniformed player or coach steals signs or "cheats" it is fair, when a "civilian" does it it is not. But knowing doesn't always help anyhow. I recall that someone on the Houston Astros learned to "read" Sandy Koufax and the whole team was able to tell when he was going to throw a curve. But Koufax was so good the information was of little practical value.

Finally, there are the nicknames. All homogeneous groups love nicknames, and baseball people use them freely. Naturally, many of the nicknames remain within the confines of the profession and are not known to the average fan who becomes familiar only with those that the sportswriters and announcers use. George Herman Ruth was called "Jidge" by most of his teammates and "The Big Monk" or "Monkey" by most of his opponents. He was "Babe" to the fans though because that is the name the newspapers used, attracted perhaps by its similarity to President Cleveland's Baby Ruth. Many nicknames are not at all complimentary and often infuriate the player involved. John McGraw hated the name "Mugsy," given to him because he looked like a Baltimore politician of dubious morals. Newsmen avoided it. Few of his players

were rash enough to call him that in his short-fused presence, for McGraw reacted to Mugsy just about as vigorously as Bill Klem reacted to Catfish. And Yankee relief pitcher Johnny Murphy, later General Manager of the Mets, was never too happy about being referred to as "Grandma" because of his particular habits.

To learn such names, the outsider has to keep his eyes and ears wide open, as most sportscasters and announcers are not out to antagonize the very persons from whom they draw their living. Sometimes, in fact, a good bit of wit has to go down the drain. Bob Chance, the rotund first baseman-outfielder who hung on the edge of the majors for a few years in the '60s, was dubbed "Fat" Chance at first. It was a great name, but it didn't sit well and was almost completely dropped by the press. On the other hand, Jay Dean was perfectly willing to capitalize on "Dizzy" and Joe Garagiola didn't worry about being "The Dago." Often the names are good-natured enough, even complimentary enough, that the player becomes sort of proud of them as the Brooklyn franchise did of Dodgers or the Pittsburgh franchise did of Pirates. Walter "Boom Boom" Beck, so-called because of the noise made by his opponents' bats whenever he was pitching, liked his nickname. Nor did Sal Maglie mind being called "The Barber." Maglie, who got the name because he was a mean pitcher who specialized in "shaving" or "brushing back" the hitters, revelled in being hard-nosed and capitalized on it.

Although now and then an "inglorious Milton" unmutes his poetic urge in these names, labelling Ted Abernathy "Angleworm" because he pitches underhand and his stuff seems to rise up out of the ground, calling, as Whitey Ford did, Pete Rose "Charley Hustle" because he sprints wher-

Rookie southpaw Sandy Koufax displays the form that took him
to pitching greatness in a 1957 Dodgers-Cubs contest.
Koufax struck out 13 Cubs as the Brooklyn club edged Chicago, 3–2.
(Wide World)

Joe Garagiola, big-league catcher turned NBC sportscaster, hams it up with cap and catcher's mask. *(Wide World)*

ever he goes on the ballfield, the bulk of the names are routine, the usual run of the locker-room in any sport: Rabbit, Hoss, Moose, Batman, Skeeter, Country, Wop, Whale-body, Four-eyes, Peanuts. Some are almost automatic: all Campbells being Soupy, all Rhodeses being Dusty. Others are brought along from pre-baseball days: Bubba Church or Dazzy Vance. Some are created in the usually vain hope of emulating an earlier star: Babe Herman or Sad Sam Jones. Others reflect a personal habit: Sloppy Thurston, who was immaculate, or Bobo Newsom, who called everyone by that Spanish term for "fool." Once in awhile the nicknames are so good and so appropriate that they replace the regular names. A lot of ball fans have to think twice to recall the actual first names of Junior Gilliam, Yogi Berra, Casey Stengel, Boog Powell, Blue Moon Odom, Mule Haas, or Goose Goslin.

Anecdotes accounting for these nicknames are bound to occur. Such stories are no more apt to be true than the pseudo-legends that account for the club names. But one can never be sure. Perhaps Harold "Muddy" Ruel really got his name after falling in a mud-puddle as a child. Perhaps Paul and Lloyd Waner, Big and Little Poison, were so-called because a writer misunderstood a Brooklyn fan's accent when he said, "Here comes that big person to bat." And Lena Blackburn really did get that name when a fan in Worcester, Massachusetts, converted his nickname "Lean" into a girl's name after he had made a great play. Lee Allen used to tell a representative and unlikely story involving the nickname of nineteenth-century umpire, "Honest John" Kelly. Kelly, it seems, was travelling with a friend one wintry night near Akron, Ohio. Their horse lost his footing in a snowdrift and bolted. Kelly and his pal leaped from the careening carriage to safety, but the horse ran on. After walking three miles to a farmhouse, Kelly knocked at the door, introduced himself, and asked the farmer if he could hire a conveyance to get back to town. The farmer replied, "I ain't never heard of ye, but ye look honest to me, John Kelly, and I'll give you a lift." Harnessing the farmer's best mare to a buckboard, Kelly put down a deposit of two dollars and agreed to bring the animal and the rig back the next day. He and his pal reached Akron safely, but the mare died in the stable before morning. The next day, Kelly returned with the farmer's rig hitched on behind his own buggy and, explaining, paid the farmer an extra $20 for the dead mare. "You're honest, John Kelly," the farmer said warmly, and that's what he was called, "Honest John" Kelly, for the rest of his days.

There is also the phoney nickname, the name made up and used by the press, but pretty well ignored in the locker rooms. A very successful name of this sort was "Joltin' Joe" or "The Jolter" for Joe DiMaggio. Through a steady use of the name in the newspapers, through a mediocre popular song with the refrain "Joltin' Joe DiMaggio, we want you on our side," and through such things as paperback books, T-shirts, and the like, Joltin'

Joe became widely known in the America of the 1940s. But even the fans never took to calling Paul Dean "Daffy" just because his far more outgoing brother was Dizzy, and it is doubtful if persons other than newspapermen and announcers referred to Babe Ruth as "Bambino," Lou Gehrig as "The Iron Horse," Bob Feller as "Rapid Robert," or Ted Williams as either "The Splendid Splinter" or, as *Sports Illustrated* coyly called him, "Teddy Ballgame."

In closing, let me point out that when one looks at the numerous contributions baseball cant and its associated areas have made to the American language, he has before him a most convincing argument that "an elaborate form of rounders" is indeed our national game. No other sport and few other occupations have introduced so many phrases, so many words, so many twists into our language as has baseball. The true test comes in the fact that old ladies who have never been to the ballpark, coquettes who don't know or care who's on first, men who think athletics begin and end with a pair of goalposts, still know and use a great deal of baseball-derived terminology. Perhaps other sports, in their efforts to replace baseball as "our national pastime," have two strikes on them before they come to bat.

George Herman (Babe) Ruth addresses Yankee Stadium crowd and the nation
during Babe Ruth Day ceremonies, April 27, 1947.
National League President Ford Frick (left of microphones),
radio announcer Mel Allen, Francis Cardinal Spellman
and baseball commissioner A. B. (Happy) Chandler look on. *(Wide World)*

FOURTH

RUTH, RUTHLESS, AND THE MAN WHO PLAYED GOD

THINK of a group of dim figures in a peculiar sort of hell. Their torture is to report day after day about people as they never were, to dramatize events that by their constant repetition have long since become routine, to give life-and-death importance to the insignificant. For tools they are given stereotyped characterizations, fads, clichés, conventionalized thought, and gullible, if not downright ignorant, readers. As time passes, they begin to believe in themselves and their role, uniting into a fraternity which is compelled to snap at the colorful, which must treat gossip as fact, which thinks people actually recall what they have to say. These are the American sportswriters. I recall Joel Sayre, an old sportswriter himself, telling me that most newsmen found it hard to remain in sports after a few, vicarious years. "They are," he said, "Chinese coolies levelling out airstrips by pounding their rocks against the ground." Yet as far as the semi-folk occupation of baseball goes, these are the mythmakers: the scops, the gleemen, the chroniclers of the profession. They are the creators of much of the lore, the embryonic legends, the heroic figures,

the speech we associate with our national game. What they don't create, they edit and transmit. Through them, the player-to-be may first learn the lore of the occupation. Through them, most of the American people get their steadiest look at baseball. Through them, the interplay of the sport and our culture takes place.

The basic idea which these scops stress is that each particular game, series, or season is of lasting importance to the world at large, that "history is being made." This formula, of necessity, is nearly sacred. Without it there would be little reason for the sportswriter's existence; without it there would be no backdrop against which the heroes of the game could stand. Yet it is all "a paper moon." For although the panorama of a sport like baseball can be of great significance in a culture, no particular incident, no particular game, no particular pennant means a damn thing. "A garland briefer than a girl's" Housman described success in athletics; and we do forget quickly, even if we were down on our knees praying about the outcome during the struggle. This combination of acute im-

65

Babe Ruth entertains some young fans with baseball anecdotes during a break in batting practice, 1932. (Wide World)

portance at the moment and almost no importance when all is done is what makes sports such a safe and useful substitute for war and the hunt. So the sportswriter's task is to be chronicler to "much ado about little," stressing the life and death aspects of something no one will or should worry about "when yesterday's gone." We might forgive

him his hell if he seemed to understand it, but he doesn't. He pounds away at his airstrip as blindly as any laborer on Kafka's Great Wall of China. It is a very sobering thought!

History at the popular level is a sobering subject anyhow. Each age re-writes the past into a drama to fit its own purposes—a statement which simply means that one never learns what actually happened or what people were actually like, only what some chronicler wants to think happened, wants to think someone was like. At the learned level, the level of the professional historian, such dramatization is done within the framework of what I have termed "secondary objectivity." That is, a man re-writes history to fit the age of which he is a part, but within that license tries conscientiously to present events and people as they actually were. Arthur Schlesinger, Jr.'s study of Andrew Jackson is a fine case in point—a study of the age of Jackson within the framework of Rooseveltian political philosophy, but nonetheless, given the slant, an attempt to be an accurate picture of the times and the man. At the folk and popular level the whole thing is without that secondary objectivity and the dramatization is crass. Events and personalities are immediately crammed into pre-conceived formulas and little worry is accorded accuracy or actuality. For example, a popular-folk formula tells us that an outlaw is a good boy wronged by oppressors, who robs the rich because they deserve it and turns his profits over to the poor. The formula is so strong that people in Missouri and Oklahoma today believe sincerely that the historical Jesse James was a fine lad and that the real Pretty Boy Floyd was committed to helping families on relief, in spite of the fact that James, at least when drunk, was a sadist and Floyd a demented killer. It is vital as we start a discussion of the popular and folk heroes of baseball that we keep these things in mind, never forgetting that sportswriters are incapable of rising beyond formulaic presentation, if not because they cannot conceive of matters in other terms, only because their readers do not want them to. So baseball heroes, strutting and fretting upon an artificial stage, find their personalities being crammed into basic stereotypes that the world seems never to have been without.

Since time immemorial man has had culture heroes: that is, mythical figures like Prometheus of the ancient Greeks, Coyote of the Plains Indians, who create the world, regulate it so that man can live in it, and teach human beings about their institutions, about sex, death, disease, food, and the like. As new religions replace old, such figures do not always die. Often, replaced as culture heroes by other demi-gods, they survive as misty historical figures who supposedly lived long-ago-lives worth emulation today, lives that hold the basic codes of conduct in focus for the society involved. Thus, culture heroes who are religious, mythological figures may become legendary, semi-historical figures. Hercules is an example. Originally, perhaps a lion-god of some Near Eastern tribe, he became a model military adventurer for the ancient Greeks, the kind of man anyone would be if he could. On the other hand, all legendary heroes are not derived from culture heroes who have lost their religious base. Some are products of history, gaining stature over the ages until, half-hidden by the fogs of time, they appear semi-divine, much like their brothers who were formerly deities.

These legendary heroes of folklore divide themselves into three general types: prowess heroes, tricksters, and ethical heroes. If the people are war-like, perhaps at the hunting-gathering level, the hero may well be nothing but a mass of strength, of crude power, courage, and determina-

The Babe donned a bushy set of whiskers for a 1933 exhibition game with the House of David team in St. Petersburg, Florida. *(Wide World)*

tion. Like Ajax and Achilles of *The Iliad* their demi-divinity, their heroic stature, will rise from sheer brawn, and they will take advantage of their superior size, speed, resistance to pain to accomplish their ends. Such heroes seldom resort to tricks or plans. They don't need to. Success lies straight ahead. The prowess hero stands in direct contrast to the trickster, the little creature like the American Negro Bre'r Rabbit or the woodland Indian Whiskey Jack who has no choice but to rely on brains and guile to better his powerful adversaries and accomplish his often amoral ends. He also contrasts to the moral teacher: the Hiawatha, the Jesus, the Moses, who never resorts to strength, who does not use guile, but who persuades and inspires. I call this latter sort of hero an ethical hero, and his job is to bring a code of conduct to the society, leaving that code as a model against which future generations can measure themselves. As I take up the baseball variants of these stereotypes in this chapter and the next, I feel obliged to divide them into the more traditional ones that are taken earnestly and the more recent, American adaptations that are comic or semi-comic. Let's start with those about whom we do not smile—with Babe Ruth, a baseball prowess hero; with Ty Cobb, a non-comic trickster; and with Judge Landis, an ethical hero. The comic variations can wait until Chapter 5.

Ruth sprung from a Baltimore orphanage baseball's prowess hero incarnate like Dionysius from Zeus' hip. Crude, animalistic, literate at the lowest level, Ruth completely dominated a generation of major-league baseball with natural talent. One of the top pitchers in the game, he became the greatest slugger of all-time. Even without the four years he spent on the mound, he established a career record of 714 roundtrippers which is so amazing that the man who surpassed it had been at bat well over 2,800 more times than the Babe. He hit over 50 homers in a season four times, and in spite of Roger Maris' 61 in a 162-game schedule, he still holds the record of 60 in a 154-game season. In 1927, when he set that record, he alone hit one-eighth of the homers hit by the American League, a ratio that demanded 150 from Maris in 1961! As Stan Musial once put it, "He was good enough to pitch and bat fourth [in the majors], like the star of a high school team. Even though he struck out more than 1300 times, he still had a career average of .341." Ruth himself claimed with appropriate braggadocio that he could have hit .600 during his entire career if he had deigned to go for opposite-field singles. And he might have come close. But, as Bob Broeg of *The Sporting News* remarked, "To try to capture Ruth with cold statistics would be like trying to keep up with him on a night out." It can't be done.

It can't be done because seeing Ruth was seeing something or someone who was the best, a bit beyond what we normally find in human beings. Ruth's batting was Titanic, in the mythological sense of that word—smooth, but memorable for raw, sheer power, nothing if not overwhelming. Nevertheless, perhaps the most remarkable thing he ever did on the ballfield was to return to pitching after a 12-year layoff at the age of 38. In the final game of the 1933 season, before 25,000 people (too few to have watched what occurred), he shut out his old team the Red Sox for 5 innings until his arm stiffened. Then, with sheer guts, he hung on to gain a victory, the 6–5 score including one of his own homers. Completely exhausted, he couldn't even raise his left hand to tip his hat to a crowd that waited for him outside the locker-room an hour after the game.

Had he done equivalent things on the "ringing plains of windy Troy," Homer would have fashioned an epic hero from him. As he did them on the ballfield, he became a mass-media Achilles. And such specimens of prowess are expected to have epic appetites to match. Ethan Allen drinks so much whiskey that a rattlesnake which bites him gets drunk. Hercules sleeps with the king's fifty daughters one after another the same night; each bears him a son, the first and last producing twins. Beowulf stands in the Court of Hrothgar and brags of his greatness, then proves it by slaying Grendel. Wine, women, words—Ruth was noticed for these things too, and what he didn't or couldn't perform on his own was quickly attributed to him by his chroniclers and peers.

So the stories are told again and again. The train comes into a Carolina town on the way north from spring training. The Babe gets out and gobbles down one, two, three dozen hotdogs and one, two, three gallons of cheap soda pop. The resultant stomach-ache is felt across the land. Pals watch aghast as Ruth orders breakfast: a pint of bourbon, quarts of ginger ale, four or five fried eggs, a pot of coffee, a side order of fried potatoes, a stack of bacon, a stack of toast. Nor does such lack of concern for training-table logic harm his athletic performance in any way. A Pittsburgh reporter tells Manager Pie Traynor not to worry about the then-forty-year-old Ruth. The reporter has had him out drinking until 5 A.M. Both smile, only to see the Babe smash three homers that afternoon, the last time he ever did it. Al Schacht and Goose Goslin conspire to ruin Ruth's series in Washington by having Goslin, a highly trained guide, give him a complete tour of nightlife

Singer Kate Smith and Babe Ruth joined forces on September 17, 1936 to create a unique radio comedy team. *(Wide World)*

in the Capitol. So well does Goslin do the job that he leaves Ruth after breakfast with a reporter who takes him sleepless to Walter Reed Hospital where he signs autographs till game-time. That afternoon, Ruth hits two homers and a double, while Goslin goes 0 for 5 and makes two errors. It matters little that the stomach-ache was either the result of one bite of one frank that had spoiled in the Dixie sun or of a hangover euphemized for delicate, if not always abstemious, readers. It matters little that hundreds

**Young infantile paralysis victims salute the Babe
with raised bats during the slugger's 1941 visit
to the Hospital for Joint Diseases.** *(Wide World)*

of athletes have eaten larger and more bizarre meals than the Babe. It matters little that Ruth was countless times sleepless or near-sleepless upon showing up at the ballpark. It matters little because the stories survive as symbols, nothing more.

Of course the American press never could stress Ruth's sexual prowess, though he was what the eighteenth century called a "great wencher." Such matters had to be approached obliquely by the chroniclers who simply indicated his amazing charm for women. Thus the Babe, sweaty and unbathed, arrives in the 100-degree midsummer heat of St. Louis after an all-night train ride. As he enters the lobby of the Chase Hotel, he is embraced by adoring females, each of whom is overwhelmed by his sexual, rather than his olfactory, animalism. But he is free to brag— as long as he makes good. He calls his shot against Charlie Root, hitting the famous "indicator" homerun. He goes to the local hospital to comfort a dying boy. At the bedside he promises to hit one that day "just for you, kid"—and he does it, while the little fellow clings to the radio, fighting through, recovering, unable to die after the god has wrought a miracle especially for him.

Insouciance is another important quality of the prowess hero. Where most people are attentive to detail, getting to know their teammates, remembering names, the hero, by his greatness, is freed from such pointless routine. So Ruth never bothers to find out who's pitching against the Yankees, for he can rip them all; never recalls the ballpark, the team, his own teammates. He's above such trivia. So a pal asks him what he thinks of the latest Yankee second baseman, Don Heffner, and the Babe has never heard of the guy. So Waite Hoyt, an old drinking

(Left to right) Babe Ruth, actor Gary Cooper, and Bill Dickey pose on Wrigley Field during the filming of "Pride of the Yankees," the Lou Gehrig story. *(Wide World)*

and wenching pal, is traded away to Philadelphia and comes to say good-bye. "Good luck, kid," says the Babe, with those inevitable tears in his eyes. "Take care of yourself, Walter." So Ruth greets President Calvin Coolidge that day in Griffith Stadium with a casual, "Geez it's hot, ain't it, Pres?" while Coolidge is forced by the rules of democratic *noblesse oblige* to let a chuckle escape from his dour face. So Ruth, with a salary grotesquely higher than that of President Hoover, is reported to have attributed the fact to his having "had a better year" than the President.

God alone knows which of the anecdotes attributed to him Ruth actually acted out and which he did not. Probably all of the anecdotes are elaborated from some kernel of truth. I firmly believe legend to be a formulaic development of historical fact. I mean Ruth did visit sick kids and maybe he did luck out by hitting a homer the same day, or the next. He did something with his hand before Root threw that 2 and 2 pitch. He was sick or hung over on the training trip north in 1925. He met Calvin Coolidge during a heat-wave. And if he didn't do some of the things attributed to him, the chances are someone else did and the incidents have gravitated to the Babe in his role as prowess hero. All heroes attract stories from lesser figures and from discarded forerunners. This is standard and has been occurring throughout history, to Hercules, to Achilles, to Ethan Allen, as well as to ballplayers.

Some of the anecdotes about Ruth were actually staged. It is one thing for a chronicler to re-write fact according to preconceived formulas or to borrow tales from similar figures and attach them to the hero in question, but it is pretty much unheard of in folk and popular lore for the chronicler to persuade the hero to perform according to formula, making as it were history occur as legend. This is something that only mass-media communications has made feasible. Today, for instance, a baseball writer who wants a hero to hit a homer for a sick kid actually has, through press influence, the ability to stage and disseminate the legend pretty much whenever he wants. Look what they did to Ruth. After the 1925 season, after the Babe had clowned, wenched, and drunk his way out of favor with Yankee manager Miller Huggins and the American public, Christy Walsh callously staged a dinner at which

Thousands of people waited in a line winding around Yankee Stadium on the night of August 17, 1948, to pay their respects to Babe Ruth, whose body was lying in state in the stadium rotunda. *(Wide World)*

Ruth's obligation to the "dirty-faced little boy in the bleachers" was the main course. The Babe was actually instructed what to do and what to say. With tears streaming down his face, he apologized to the kids of America, right after Mayor Jimmy Walker had given him a public dressing down worthy of a school-marm. This is now one of the most famous of the Ruth "legends"—how the freckle-faced kids of this great land brought the errant hero to his senses. Medieval historians, chroniclers, were among the crassest fabricators historiography has ever known, yet next to some of the twentieth century's "tub thumpers" they really do appear to be saints.

Ruth is the game's one fully developed prowess hero, but he is not the only physical specimen whose career has been tinged with the legendary. The hospital story occurs regularly with Lou Gehrig, Ted Williams, Willie Mays, anybody of the moment, in the main role. But, for one reason or another, none of the rest has really challenged Ruth's pre-eminence. Lou Gehrig's case is typical. An excellent hitter, he played and is recalled in Ruth's shadow. Few, for instance, remember that he followed the "indicator" home run with one of his own. Today, people know but two things about him: one, he set a colorless record by "iron-horsing" his way through 2130 consecutive games from June 2, 1925, to May 2, 1939; and two, his career and life were cut short by amytrophic lateral sclerosis. An honest, clean-cut, but publicly bland person, Gehrig was developed first by the sportswriters and later by Hollywood as a tragic figure, the warrior cut off in his prime. He did give a moving speech to a crowded Yankee Stadium when honored there just before his death. Nonetheless, although most Americans recognize his name, they do so

"The home run twins," Babe Ruth and Lou Gehrig, walk to the Yankee dugout after both scored on Gehrig's homer in the first game of the 1932 World Series. *(Wide World)*

73

CHARLES DILLON STENGEL
"CASEY"

MANAGED NEW YORK YANKEES 1949-1960.
WON 10 PENNANTS AND 7 WORLD SERIES WITH
NEW YORK YANKEES. ONLY MANAGER TO WIN
5 CONSECUTIVE WORLD SERIES 1949-1953.
PLAYED OUTFIELD 1912-1925 WITH BROOKLYN,
PITTSBURGH, PHILADELPHIA, NEW YORK AND
BOSTON N.L. TEAMS. MANAGED BROOKLYN
1934-1936. BOSTON BRAVES 1938-1943.
NEW YORK METS 1962-1965.

THEODORE SAMUEL WILLIAMS
"TED"

BOSTON RED SOX A.L. 1939-1960
BATTED .406 IN 1941. LED A.L. IN BATTING
6 TIMES; SLUGGING PERCENTAGE 9 TIMES;
TOTAL BASES 6 TIMES; RUNS SCORED 6 TIMES;
BASES ON BALLS 8 TIMES. TOTAL HITS 2654
INCLUDED 521 HOME RUNS. LIFETIME BATTING
AVERAGE .344; LIFETIME SLUGGING AVERAGE
.634. MOST VALUABLE A.L. PLAYER 1946 & 1949.
PLAYED IN 18 ALL STAR GAMES. NAMED PLAYER
OF THE DECADE 1951-1960.

**Plaques honoring Charles Dillon (Casey) Stengel and Ted Williams
were dedicated at the Baseball Hall of Fame in 1966.** *(Wide World)*

74

within this sentimental rather than within any truly heroic context.

Ted Williams, on the other hand, ruined his chances for legendary heroism by carrying on a personal vendetta with both the "chroniclers" and the adoring masses. As gifted and dedicated a hitter as ever came into the majors, Williams was emotionally so immature during the bulk of his career that he acted like a selfish, spoiled kid a lot of the time, vacillating as such people will between charm and tantrums. Such behavior might not have hurt him, certainly immaturity was no drawback to Ruth, except for one thing: unlike Ruth, who was essentially likeable, Williams was intense, too believable in his unhappy moments. Where, deep down, no one took Ruth's antics seriously, Williams' indiscretions were utterly in earnest. Crude as Ruth was, it was not in his make-up to hold mass grudges or to "give the crowd the finger."

Williams had another characteristic that hurt him almost as much as his peevishness. He was utterly scientific about his hitting. The anecdote about the final game of the 1949 season is most indicative. This game, between the Red Sox and the Yankees, was for the pennant. It was tense, a pitching duel between Vic Raschi and Ellis Kinder. In the seventh, Williams came to bat with the tying run on base. With the count 3 and 2, Raschi threw a careful curve that broke just outside. Williams, who had stubbornly trained himself never to swing at a bad pitch, let it go and walked. Vern Stephens followed him, popping up to end the threat; and when the Yankees went on to win both the game and the pennant, Williams was roasted by the second-guessers. They accused him of choking, of not daring to swing, of leaving matters up to Stephens. Even

Raschi was reported to have been surprised that Williams would let that pitch go in that situation. Of course what everyone was saying was that the hero must have a bit of the fool in him. Williams was correct. A batter should never widen his strike zone by swinging at bad pitches. But heroes aren't the products of logic. Heroes swing at just such pitches, dramatically, willy-nilly, and convert them into victories, never considering percentages or what fools they will seem should they fail.

Nonetheless, Williams will always be remembered for the fantastic eyesight that made him one of the shrewdest judges of balls and strikes ever to go to the plate. There is a legendary atmosphere about the stories of how well he could see. They tell how he was called out on strikes, objected to the umpire, and was later proved right by movies taken of the pitch. It has been told that he could see ducks flying toward the blind long before the other hunters knew they were coming. Even though he has denied the fact, most people believe he could read the label on a spinning 78 rpm phonograph record. And Arthur Daley in a *Times* column of February 25, 1969, insisted that Williams was able to recognize him at once from across a spring training field, even though Daley and his friends couldn't identify a single person as they blinked back. There is no doubt the man does have fantastic eyesight, but that is not the point. The point is that people account for his having been able to hit better than most batters should by exaggerating that eyesight. There is an urge toward legend here, but one that will probably never bloom farther than it has.

The concept of the prowess hero is relatively simple. That of the trickster is more complex, for that matter quite paradoxical. The trickster may be of divine importance, acting as culture hero, creating and ordering the world, instructing humanity how to behave; but he may also be a fool or clown, demonstrating what man should not do, acting out silly, stupid roles often harmful to himself and his own, sometimes rebelling against the very institutions he has helped create. Often he is just a prankster, involved in harmless hoaxes, complicating situations, perhaps the

main character in a cycle of jokes. Whatever his role in any particular tale in any particular culture he is nearly always without brawn, living by his wits and resourcefulness. Roger Abrahams has described him as follows in a Voice of America broadcast:

His outstanding characteristic is his lack of morals. As Radin says, "He wills nothing consciously. At all times he is constrained to behave as he does from impulses over which he has no control. . . . He possesses no values, moral or social, [and] is at the mercy of his passions and appetites." Yet the stories about him exist in communities with ethical values; though he represents amorality, he does so in a moral context. His actions must be condemned at the same time that they are laughed at and admired. As the enemy of constraint, he seems to function as a representative of the lawless, indeed anarchistic, aspect of ourselves which exists in even the most social creatures.

As the classicist, Karl Kerenyi, says of Trickster, he is the very "spirit of disorder, the enemy of boundaries." Essentially, we seem to be fascinated by him because he represents the principle of pure unbridled energy, directed into human shape and impelled by primal human needs. But this only explains about half of the stories about Trickster, those in which he actively dupes others. But as often as not, he tricks himself. And when he does so, his exploits are nothing less than clownish and his mask is that of the noodle, the simpleton.

Willie Mays slides safely into home as Cubs catcher Forrest Burges lunges at him with the ball, too late to make the out. Willie took off from third as Cubs' Frank Miller pitched to Giants' Wes Westrum (left). (Wide World)

Modern man, with his systematic, scientific mind, does not find the primitive trickster an easy creature to understand. He is too unmotivated, perhaps too uncontrollable for our level of civilization. Thus, where we have preserved the trickster, we have relegated him to comedy or to cycles of jokes where paradox, selfish whimsy, and lack of motivation can be tolerated. When asked to take him seriously we are afraid of him, troubled by him, and we tend to discard him if we can.

Baseball has produced but one trickster who is neither clown nor semi-clown: Ty Cobb. A top-flight player for over 23 years, producer of 4191 basehits, with an exceptional lifetime batting average of .367, Cobb is usually considered the best of the oldtimers, next to Ruth the greatest player who ever lived. Remarkable as he may seem, it is certain in these days of night-games, scoop-like gloves, solid pitching staffs, relief hurlers, and greater depth of talent, he could not have been what he was, nor created the image that he created. He symbolizes the days before the slugger Ruth when baseball was played close to the vest and featured the steal, the hit-and-run, the extra base on the throw—elements that while still important have been eclipsed by the simple power of a mighty swing with a souped-up bat against a souped-up ball.

Tyrus Raymond Cobb was born in the pitch-pine country of Georgia in a town called Narrows. Spurning family hopes that he would end up a lawyer or a general, he gravitated toward professional baseball with a 5' 10", 155-pound frame. Released by Augusta in his first trial, he gave it another shot with the maxim "Don't come home a failure" ringing in his ears. With the help of a minor league manager, George Leidy, endless hours of practice, salmon-like determination, and growth that brought his height up to 6' 1" and his weight to near 190, he "came home" a huge success. Unhappily it was to a mother who had shot to death "a prowler," a sometime State Senator and Superintendent of County Schools, her own husband, trying to surprise her with her lover.

Ty Cobb strikes a pose. The great old-time outfielder's career spanned the years 1905–1928. (*Wide World*)

No, Ty Cobb's not balancing that huge baseball atop his balding dome. The sphere is part of the background decorations for the ceremony inducting Jerome Herman (Dizzy) Dean and Al Simmons into baseball's Hall of Fame. *(Wide World)*

Either through this environmental background or through inheritance, young Cobb's personality soon developed "that illness" which Lady MacBeth claims "should attend ambition," and once he had learned the mechanics of his business, he became the most ornery, crafty, win-at-all-costs player who ever put on spikes. Not that there isn't much about him to admire. Old and wealthy, he built a medical center in honor of his unfortunate dad, endowed a foundation to help youngsters through college, took care of George Leidy when he was down and out. Anyone who practices bunting hour after hour by trying to lay the ball on a blanket spread along the basepaths, who slides again and again till his legs are raw, who wears lead weights in his shoes to make his spikes feel lighter during the game, who continues to do these things long after he has hit the top, throughout a major league career which stretched from 1905 to 1928, is remarkable. So is someone who is competitive enough to play and play well with his legs bleeding and bruised, his ribs cracked, his temperature at 103°. But there was not enough of this in the face of all the ruthlessness, trickiness, and pugnacity. For Cobb was a ballplayer so "ill" in the Shakespearian sense, he was almost a fanatic. An anecdote dating from 1905 in Augusta when he roomed with Nap Rucker shows his lack of proportion. Insisting that Rucker let him shower first, he supposedly shouted, "I mean, Nap, I've got to be first all the time—first in everything!" His trigger-temper, cause of a long series of fist fights with fans, umpires, and teammates, sometimes even with men like huge Germany Schmidt who twice beat him to a pulp because he wouldn't quit, is almost like that of a wolverine.

And out of this illness the legends begin to grow,

creating Cobb as a man never to be aroused, never to be crossed, a man made up of only fury, iced-blood, and a thousand devices. Cobb thus becomes a creature without normal motivation, a ballplayer, like some primitive trickster, who goes about his business of victory oblivious to the laws and customs of the society in which he lives. Where Ruth, almost good-naturedly, slammed out a homer to win the day, Cobb, with less strength, accomplished triumph with craft and intensity. Unable to cope with Billy Sullivan's throwing arm, he announces he will steal on the second pitch. Sullivan, wondering whether to believe him or not, becomes sufficiently troubled to give Cobb the edge he needs. Later in the same game, he repeats the statement but takes off on the first pitch. Unable to hit Walter Johnson's fastball, he crowds the plate so that Johnson, who lived in fear he might kill someone with his speed, throws balls rather than skull this apparently foolish batter. When Johnson gets behind on the count, Cobb either slaps a hit off "the cripple" or waits out a walk. The most appropriate example of this sort of legend relates how the trickster Cobb defeats the powerful Ruth, reduced for the purposes of the plot from prowess hero to slow-thinking bear. Managing from centerfield, Cobb, according to a pre-conceived plan, signals the pitcher to give Ruth an intentional walk. Ruth relaxes and takes a strike right down the pipe. Cobb rushes in from the outfield and chews out the seemingly moronic pitcher. The next pitch is also down the pipe. Cobb goes into a frenzy, yanking both the pitcher and the catcher, shouting at them that they are fined $100 apiece. A new battery is brought in and clearly instructed to walk Ruth intentionally. The new pitcher throws a couple of balls, lulling Ruth back to sleep, and

Seventy-five-year-old Ty Cobb and then–New York State Governor Nelson A. Rockefeller playfully "choose up sides" with the silver bat awarded Cobb at the 1960 Baseball Writers' Association Dinner for having batted .420 during the 1911 season. Rockefeller was a guest at the dinner. *(Wide World)*

then whips over the third strike, sending the Babe back to the dugout like Bre'r Bear in a Joel Chandler Harris story.

But like all tricksters, Cobb never works without knowing the percentages and the background of the situation. He is aware of Sullivan's imagination, of Johnson's fears, of

Ruth's slow mind. He wouldn't try such tricks on a catcher who was too dumb to be fooled, on a Carl May-type pitcher who would dust his own mother, on a crafty batter like Napoleon Lajoie. For example, he answers Lou Criger's publicized boast that no one can run on him by stealing five bases, including third and home, even holding up the game at one point to announce when he will take off. But he does this because he knows that he can get a huge jump on the fellow pitching and that Criger doesn't have a prayer.

And when guile wouldn't serve, Cobb always felt fury could do it. Like a bull sparrow, he figured he had more determination, resistance to pain, and sheer guts than other players. So he spiked or threatened to spike infielders; bowled over catchers when it wasn't necessary; stole bases to practice for the day when a steal might win a game —stoking the reputation that might cause a man here to flinch, a man there to worry.

He allowed no one close to him. A loner in baseball, he was a loner throughout most of his life. Two women divorced him. Most of the players hated his guts. In 1910, some of them even conspired to give the batting title to Napoleon Lajoie rather than let him win it. But this is the way with non-comic tricksters, for their role in the scheme of things is amoral, antisocial, a model of what not to do as often as of what to do. A non-comic trickster behaves as we all would behave if we were not constrained by convention and timidity—and while we are fascinated with him because of it, we are afraid of him too. It is the prowess hero, or better yet the ethical hero, that our society best understands—although neither are quite as exciting.

In a Judeo-Christian society there is little room for a genuine ethical hero. Religious figures like Christ and Moses have assumed that role. Ethical heroes, where they arise in our folklore, arise in the secular parts of life, particularly in law and politics where they establish their codes of conduct, inviting respect and emulation. Think of Benjamin Franklin, Abraham Lincoln—and Roy Bean.

Roy Bean was born in Kentucky in 1825. He went west "with the country" and eventually became the Justice of the Peace in Langtry, Texas. Setting up his own court in his own "The Jersey Lily Saloon," he called himself "The Law West of the Pecos" and ran an arbitrary, casual, dishonest, and often vicious bench. He claimed to use the laws of California for his judgments, even though Texas had its own codes and statutes, saying what was good enough for one area was good enough for another. Actually, it made little difference. Frequently there were no "lawyers" for the defense; the "jury" and the defendants, to say nothing of the judge, were likely to be drunk. Bean ruled on cases alone, his pronouncements whimsical and final, sometimes deciding life and death. Most often, however, he simply lined his own pockets, calling "court to order" to fine customers $20 for "disturbing the peace," when they objected to paying $1 for a glass of beer or bringing suit at his own bench, then awarding damages to himself, assessing the defendant "court costs" which usually meant "drinks all around." Time has made his shenanigans semi-comic and elaborated on them. It is doubtful if the historical Bean was comic at all. A colorful petty tyrant, yes, but a figure those involved with would not care to laugh about.

Bean may seem a strange companion for Benjamin

Franklin and Abraham Lincoln, and certainly he does not leave a formal doctrine as did Christ or Moses. But his way of doing things forms a kind of "code of justice" that hosts of Americans have followed, and he does symbolize that code. Bean operated in "the old way": the lord of the feudal manor who settled peasant disputes willy-nilly; the chief of the West African tribe who decided which party had told the best proverb and so won the case; the captain of the ship who sentenced the sailor to keelhauling for talking back—a method of arbitration that right or wrong is ever clear-cut. Modern America has been slowly discarding "Roy Bean justice" in its efforts to be really fair, democratic, and unbiased. Yet at the beginning of *The Great Gatsby* when Nick Carraway looks back over the story of callousness, amorality, and insouciance that he is about to tell and states,

Conduct may be founded on the hard rock or the wet marshes, but after a certain point I don't care what it's founded on. When I came back from the East last autumn I felt that I wanted the world to be in uniform and at a sort of moral attention forever. . . .

"There is no joy in Mudville," judging by the expression on the face of Baseball Commissioner Judge Kenesaw Mountain Landis in this 1936 photo. *(Wide World)*

he is expressing a point of view associated with the Midwestern and Southern towns, with conservative, isolationist, vigilante America. It is a point of view a great many Americans still cherish, although they may be called out-of-date in doing so.

However, in the first half of the century America as a whole was closer to its nineteenth-century, rural ways and so more universally willing to accept the necessity of standing at "moral attention." It was not loath to embrace a man who would order "the world" to do so, especially in the face of "radical" pressures and minority appease-

ment on the one side, "robber baron" greed on the other. With his country accent, his snow-white hair, string ties, and penchant for cursing, Kenesaw Mountain Landis was a Latter-Day Roy Bean. Educated in a somewhat informal manner; short-fused, but a soft touch; a hater of minority groups, socialists, and communists; a VFW-type patriot, he appealed to the conservative, the traditional, the old-fashioned who found him a square bastion against the rioters, city slickers, and pay-off boys of megalopolitan life. And he did take the American law into his own hands, distributing his version of justice in the most ancient of ways.

Judge Kenesaw Mountain Landis (front row) is flanked
by American League President William Harrige (left)
and National League President Ford Frick at a 1938 "summit conference"
called to finalize World Series arrangements. Officials of several
teams stand behind the three baseball czars. *(Wide World)*

His early career is classic American, as satisfactory as that of either Franklin or Lincoln. Born in Millville, Ohio, on November 20, 1866, he was named after a Georgia mountain where his father, a Civil War surgeon, had been wounded amputating a soldier's leg. He grew up in Indiana, and his early life was typical of a small-town—odd jobs, work as a reporter for the local paper, a career as an amateur and semi-pro ballplayer, failure to finish high school. The turning point came when he decided to teach himself shorthand in order to become stenographer for the local court. This he did, and from work at the court got the desire to attend law school. With some effort he went through the Union College of Law in Chicago and began practice in the city. When Walter Q. Gresham, who had been the colonel in old Dr. Landis' regiment, was named Secretary of State under Cleveland, he took Kenesaw Mountain with him as private secretary. In Washington, in spite of his already crotchety, capricious nature, he made excellent contacts and was in 1905 appointed U.S. District Justice of the Northern District of Illinois by Teddy Roosevelt. It was in this position that his colorful ways came first to local and then to national prominence.

The case that really made him was one involving Government charges that Standard Oil of Indiana had taken freight rebates from the Chicago and Alton R.R. He handled this case just as he had been handling less prominent matters, taking complete charge, treating the lawyers, the witnesses, and the press cavalierly: assuming without hesitation the position of defense attorney, prosecutor, or technical expert; putting on a dramatic show. The press loved it, playing up the idea of the country justice versus the octopus-like corporation. Landis never disappointed them, even ordering John D. Rockefeller, Sr. to appear in court and climaxing the affair by assessing Standard Oil the staggering sum of $29,240,000. When word "leaked" out that on the very day on which he had fined Standard Oil, this country judge had also ruled for a petty loan shark who was trying to collect interest from a victim, then paid the amount from his own pocket while cursing the usurer out of court, the whole show climaxed like a Midwestern dream-come-true. Landis found himself a public hero.

Of course professional lawyers and other judges looked dubiously upon his methods. Many of his posse-type decisions, including the ruling against Standard Oil, were reversed. However, such grumblings and such reversals only served to increase his reputation as a moral rock in the marshes of modern corruption. Grumblings indicated irritation that Landis was not playing ball with the shysters; reversals indicated that the money-boys had gotten their cases out of an honest court into the hands of those judges who could be bought off. Nor did his obvious dislike of labor unions, the IWW in particular, and all such hammer and sickle, ethnic troublemakers hurt him a bit. When higher courts overturned his rulings against radical peoples and groups, the public simply saw the reversals as examples that the intellectuals were sending the world to pot and ruin. And every time a threat was made to bomb Landis' court or mail him a stick of dynamite, the public applauded his fearlessness and his stand for "the good, old country way of doing things."

He came to baseball's attention in 1916 when he examined and dismissed the Federal League's suit against Organized Ball (the National and American Leagues). A lifelong baseball fan, a former player once good enough to have turned pro, he did an immense amount of research into the game and the situation in preparation for the case. However, his ruling, correct as it might have been, was colorful and arbitrary, rather than legalistic. The Court's "expert knowledge of baseball," he stated, "obtained by more than 30 years' observation," indicates that the Federal League's suit would be "if not destructive, at least vitally injurious to the game." Actually, the case was settled out of court, but Landis' remarks were just what the National and American Leagues had wanted to hear.

Three years later the Chicago White Sox were involved in the famous World Series fix, the "Black Sox Scandal." There is no point in going into the complexities and nuances of that fix here. Leo Katcher, for one, has given it full treatment in his *The Man Who Fixed the Series*. Suffice it to emphasize one of the points he makes, that

. . . baseball ranked with love of mother and respect for the flag as untouchable. It was the "Great American Game." Its stars were among the folk heroes of the age. A man who would trifle with the honor of the game was a Benedict Arnold.

Nick Carraway, again in *The Great Gatsby*, sums up public opinion. He meets Meyer Wolfsheim, the gambler whom Fitzgerald modelled on Arnold Rothstein, a major force in the 1919 scandal.

"Fixed the World's Series?" I repeated. The idea staggered me. I remembered, of course, that the World's Series had been fixed in 1919, but if I had thought of it at all I would have thought of it as a thing that merely happened, the end of some inevitable chain. It never occurred to me that one man could start to play with the faith of fifty million people—with the singlemindedness of a burglar blowing a safe.

At any rate, through the disjointed efforts of pitcher Eddie Cicotte, first baseman Chuck Gandil, boxer Abe Attell, and gamblers Joseph "Sport" Sullivan, Bill Burns, William Maharg, and Rothstein, a rather sloppy, half-baked fix came off, and public faith in the "national game" was dealt a staggering blow. Eight players, five regulars, two top pitchers, and the utility infielder who was scouting the Cincinnati Reds were charged with involvement. Of the group, five admitted, one way or another, this involvement; two made no statement at all; and only Buck Weaver, the third baseman, actively denied his participation. Baseball, deep in a moral quagmire, was in need of a rock. And Landis was a rock, indeed.

He was hired by the clubowners to take charge of them and restore the name of the game. This he did, using the same cavalier methods that had made his reputation. At once, he banned the eight White Sox players from organized ball for life. The ruling included Buck Weaver who went to his grave insisting on his innocence and who on more than one occasion asked the Judge to reconsider. In everything, he was opinionated, firm, and final. Because of this, baseball immediately recovered from the scandal, and so thorough was the recovery that today, over 50 years later, it is still the one sport in which even the most cynical have trust.

At the beginning of the 1944 article on Landis in *Current Biography*, there is the following quotation,

Judge Kenesaw Mountain Landis, baseball's seventy-eight-year-old Commissioner, is the only successful dictator in United States history. There is no recourse from his decisions; answerable to no one, he can impose any fine or punishment he wishes for failing to obey any rule he sets for the industry which employs him.

There is little question this sophisticated version of Roy Bean served baseball as an ethical hero. And as is the case with many such heroes, his reputation for integrity and wisdom has long since outrun his reputation for whimsy, cantakerousness, and extra-legality. Only specialists recall that Congress tried to impeach Landis when he retained his seat on the bench after becoming Commissioner. Forgotten are such bizarre decisions as the one which freed an Ottawa bank clerk from a charge of embezzling $96,500 while working on a salary of $90 a week, a decision handed down with the opinion that tight-fisted employers were to blame for such crimes anyhow. Forgotten are his hate of left-of-center politics, his American Legion view of international affairs, his "Waspish" nature (in every possible nuance of those letters). Remembered are the fact that he wouldn't let a baseball owner keep a string of racehorses; that he brought Leo the Lip into line when his antics were giving the game unfavorable publicity; that he withstood Phil Ball's efforts to challenge in court his right to rule the owners, Ball included, with an iron hand. To the average American, Landis is simply the man who told baseball how it should act, proclaimed and exercised his own list of commandments, spoke his sermons from the mount of the Commissioner's office, and guided the game off the primrose path that was leading it straight to Hell.

This demi-god died in office in November 1944. Americans may be too sophisticated to suggest that Landis, like the traditional ethical heroes, has not really passed away, but has gone to some diamond-shaped Avalon to await the time when baseball will need him again, when he will descend to lead the game to a new righteousness. But there has been an aura of this about the criticism levelled at his successors:

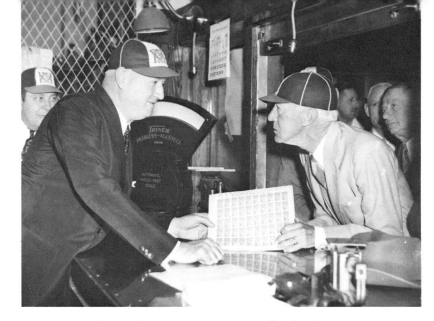

Postmaster General James A. Farley sells the first stamps commemorating baseball's centennial to Judge Kenesaw Mountain Landis in Cooperstown, New York, on June 12, 1939. (Wide World)

Happy Chandler, Ford Frick, and William Eckert. The ever-present implication has been that Judge Landis would not let the game go to pot "as it is clearly doing," that Judge Landis would keep TV and the money-mad owners in line—that Judge Landis would do something. Yet there is no role for Judge Landis in a television-oriented, minority-conscious, mid-century America, especially in a game that has become as big a business as Standard Oil itself. And there was true relief in baseball when the ancient demigod passed out of this world. He couldn't have been fired. You don't buy Moses or Christ or even Roy Bean out of their contracts. Yet by 1944 a new era was about to dawn, and while it is the ultimate tribute to Landis that it took the owners a quarter of a century to see just what sort of fellow might replace him, it is significant that when their eyes cleared of the celestial glow they picked a slick, organization-minded, PR-type Commissioner, a man better suited to the megalopolis than to vigilante justice or a "Jersey Lily Saloon."

The Chicago White Sox engage in close order drill
during 1918 spring training, under the direction
of an Army sergeant (right). *(New York Public Library)*

FIFTH

COUNTRY BOYS AND
YANKEE MERCHANTS

WHILE the prowess hero, the trickster, and the ethical hero continue to flourish in remarkably pure forms, our culture has also subjected them to some equally remarkable transformations. The most important are those that occurred in the pulp literature of the early and mid-nineteenth century with the development of the shrewd Yankee and tall-tale roarer. This literature, some of which was genuine folk literature and some of which is composed bric-a-brac, deals with a series of picaresque, footloose characters who symbolize a country torn loose from its roots, ever expanding. Continually operating on the edge of the law, they swap dead mules for live horses, water whiskey, shoot tin cups from each other's heads, fill jumping toads with buckshot, and grab ducks in mid-flight, able to transcend immorality and amorality by sheer enthusiasm, good nature, and the ever-present fact that one doesn't take what has been related as a serious threat to society or even as something that actually happened. Originally rural, then frontier, later urban in setting, such tales make up a form of legend that is distinct in that it is not believed by the teller or by knowing listeners. Such tales frequently take in the gullible, however, and serve to initiate greenhorns or to mock outsiders. Brash, blustering, fast-moving, these American yarns are always essentially comic.

Sportswriters, steeped, perhaps without knowing it, in the casual literature of the last 150 years, have consistently turned to Yankee and tall-tale stereotypes in chronicling baseball: the sage merchant, the clever clown, the frontier braggart, the country promoter, the "Marster and John" Negro all appearing again and again in the legends of our national game.

The oldest of these American stereotypes is the shrewd Yankee. Developed as a variation on the British jest-book wags, the Yankee was initially a New England comic trickster, who later finds his way west with the country. Benjamin A. Botkin in his *Treasury of New England Folklore* describes the stereotype Yankee as "sensible, self-dependent, God-fearing, freedom-loving, conservative, stubborn, practical, thrifty, industrious, inventive, and acquisitive." Originally a neighborhood swapper and sharp merchant, he soon becomes a cracker-barrel philosopher as well, as often as not disguising his wit behind a clownish exterior. As this figure spread through folk and popular literature, a certain atmosphere of unscrupulousness and

87

Brooklyn Dodgers President Branch Rickey arrives in St. Petersburg, Florida, for a hearing before Baseball Commissioner Happy Chandler. *(Wide World)*

opportunism attaches itself to his activities. But one can't afford to take his "bites" or "the coneys" he trepans seriously. When that happens, and his pranks cease to be harmless, you have little more than a shyster or outright crook.

In the world of baseball, the general manager is the one most apt to conceive of himself as a cracker-barrel merchant, swapping players (which he may call "horseflesh"), always attempting to unload a nag for a real stayer. Of the men who have assumed this image, Branch Rickey stands supreme—to borrow Thomas Carlyle's remark about Ben Franklin, "the father of all the Yankees." Like most legendary heroes, he was a natural. Born in Stockdale, Ohio, of farming parents, he fits Botkin's description of the Yankee stereotype to a "T." Of Wesleyite background, he never drank, seldom swore, and confined his smoking to cigars. During his entire life he kept a family custom of not working on Sunday, refusing to play baseball or to manage it on the Sabbath. With a country education, much of it self-given, he worked his way through Ohio Wesleyan University and eventually through Michigan Law School, using baseball, and football until he broke his leg, to pay the way. After his graduation from Ohio Wesleyan in 1906, he got a shot at the majors as a catcher, moving from Dallas to the Cincinnati Reds, who decided to release him when he refused to play on Sundays. Later he caught for the White Sox, Browns, and Highlanders, never with more than mediocre success. While at Michigan Law School, he coached the baseball team and is generally given credit for "discovering" George Sisler there. After a bout with tuberculosis and a brief try at practicing law in Boise, Idaho, Rickey began what was to be a lifelong career as baseball scout, manager, and front office man, moving from a job as

West Coast scout for the St. Louis Browns to positions as Club Secretary, Field Manager, Vice-President and Business Manager. In 1917 he was named President of the St. Louis Cardinals, though he had to go to court to get Phil Ball to release him from his Browns contract. In 1942 he moved to the Brooklyn Dodgers and in 1950, aging fast, was hired by John Galbreath and the Pittsburgh Pirates. He died in 1965.

Rickey's fame as a baseball brain, the legend of his Yankee wiliness, industry, and sagacity, develops during the period with the Cardinals. Besides innovating blackboard talks, sliding pits, and many now standard pick-off plays, he began the farm system. Operating an organization that was so poor that it couldn't afford spring training, where the team used the same uniforms on the road as at home, where he had to distribute his own salary to meet the payroll, he found necessity mothering his inventiveness. A canny judge of players, with a real knack for spotting prospects in the raw, he realized that minor league officials were earmarking athletes he showed an interest in and selling them to clubs who could pay higher prices. As a result, he came up with the idea of the farm system, by which a major league team purchases a series of minor league clubs outright or enters into working agreements with them. Starting with Houston of the Texas League and Fort Smith of the Western Association, Rickey pushed this concept to the extreme, at one time controlling the entire player supply in the Nebraska State and Arkansas-Missouri Leagues. And even though Judge Landis, who disliked the whole idea, eventually restricted major league franchises to one working agreement per league, by 1940, Rickey's "chain gang" consisted of 32 farm clubs and eight working

agreements. Under such a system, he could not only apply his ability of spotting a prospect, but he could protect that prospect until the Cardinals could use or trade him. Furthermore, Rickey had another valuable knack. He had learned how to recognize signs that a star was getting over the hill before others were aware of it. Thus, he was able to make shrewd deals—trading stars that were about to fade, filling the gaps with the rich supply of young talent, using the surplus of the farm system to deal for that one

Jackie Robinson (right) signs contract with the Montreal Royals, a Brooklyn Dodgers farm club, to become the first Black player in organized baseball in 1945. Branch Rickey, Jr., looks on over Robinson's shoulder. *(Wide World)*

established player who would insure the pennant. Consequently he was a most successful trader, and a good many general managers were "burned" by him. Nor did his habit of being slightly pontifical, aphoristic, and long-winded detract from his reputation. His conversations, as well as his speeches, were salted with cracker-barrel saws such

Jackie Robinson talks with Robert L. Finch, assistant to Brooklyn Dodgers President Branch Rickey, shortly after reporting for spring training with the Montreal Royals of the Dodgers farm system in 1946. *(Wide World)*

as "It's the history of this country that men are what they make themselves. Your education never stops"; "Look for the best in everybody, but don't allow first impressions to sway you"; "Nine times out of ten a man fashions his own destiny. You only get out of life what you put into it"; "Discipline should come from within and be self-imposed. It's more effective that way." By talking in circles, so clouding his real motives and avoiding matters he didn't want to discuss, yet quick-of-tongue and concise when he needed to be, the bushy-browed Rickey gave every impression of being wiser than he was, and his reputation for sagacity grew until he became a sort of archetype to whom all general managers looked up: the Mahatma, master of the horseflesh marts.

Rickey was notoriously tight with his players. With a farm system full of hot prospects behind him, driven by memories of Cardinal poverty, loving a good wrangle over money, he conned his charges into lower salaries and token raises, confounding their semi-educated minds with aphorisms, the mysteries of statistics, and their natural insecurity. In *Baseball Is a Funny Game* Joe Garagiola says that negotiating "a contract with Mr. Branch Rickey was like being in on the signing of the Declaration of Independence while taking a course in human behavior." He quotes Chuck Connors, later a movie star, as saying, "It was easy to figure out Mr. Rickey's thinking about contracts. He had both players and money—and just didn't like to see the two of them mix."

Economics was behind most of his moves, and I am cynical enough to be convinced that economics was the main motive behind his breaking of the color line. It was coming anyway, Rickey or not. Before World War II, baseball was a sport controlled and run by "amateurs," literally by men who loved it, most of them from lower middle class ethnic or rural backgrounds. These men gave their entire lives to the sport, happy in what profit they could get from it, but content even if no real money came their way. Such people, a high percentage of whom still discriminate against the Negroes, could indulge in their exclusiveness and think no more about it. Sure, once in awhile a John McGraw, eager enough to win, slipped a "Cuban" or an "Indian" into the line-up, but generally the game was content to let the Blacks, no matter how talented, play in their own leagues.

However, after World War II, with the growth of other professional sports, the rise in leisure time, the rise in costs, the migration of more and more Negroes to the northern and western cities, television, and the entrance of hard-core businessmen into the ownership of franchises, discrimination no longer made dollars or sense. Desire for increased markets, need for more players to stock the teams competing with football and basketball for athletes, the prospect of expansion and rival leagues, the cost-account mentality of the new-breed owner, the general atmosphere that was leading to civil rights legislation, all combined to foretell the end of baseball's discrimination. Rickey, perhaps with the same instinct that let him know when a star was "over the hill," sniffed the air and decided to be first —happy no doubt to be altruistic, but certainly sensitive to the economics of the matter.

Satch winds up . . . Leroy (Satchel) Paige pitching for the Miami Marlins against the Montreal Royals in a 1956 minor league contest. *(Wide World)*

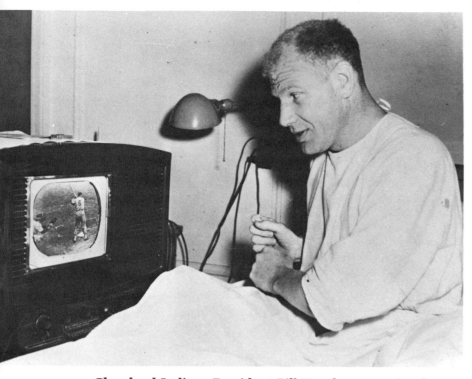

Cleveland Indians President Bill Veeck, recovering from a leg operation, watches the first telecast of a major league ballgame from Cleveland Stadium in 1948. *(UPI)*

There is no point in going over the details of his bringing Jackie Robinson to the National League. The story has been told so many times. Suffice it to say that Rickey approached the problem with the same canniness which he used in putting the Cardinals on their feet. When the initial phase of the matter was over, and what a success it turned out to be, Rickey was a hero—his Yankee acumen having brought him not only the image of the sharp swapper and local sage, but also that of Christian soldier. It's not unlike the phenomenon of Ben Franklin who parlayed his early concern with profit, loss, and maxims into a reputation for "do-good." Not that it matters. Economics is a time-honored and most effective method of motivation, and even if Rickey was not as altruistic as the mass media have made him, both Blacks and Whites are the better for it all.

As the American frontier moved west, the Yankee merchant went along, entering the backwoods where he met and fused with the heroes of the tall tales. These figures, who were scouts, meat-hunters, bargemen, added an element of boisterousness, physical violence, and braggadocio to the shrewdness and humor of the Yankee. It was as though a broad comic prowess hero had been bred with a playful trickster, the result being strong, rough, but good-humored and harmless rather than vicious. These are the roarers like Mike Fink and Davy Crockett, the pitchmen like Phineas T. Barnum, actors out of adventures too tall to be fully believed, too much fun to be dismissed.

Where the traditional Yankee is conservative, thrifty, and God-fearing, the Barnum-like promoter is loud, willing to spend in order to profit, and at best amoral. Phineas T. Barnum himself was originally a Yankee from Connecticut who began his success story by passing off an eighty-year-old Negress as George Washington's 161-year-old childhood nurse. By charging admission to see her after he purchased her for $1000, Barnum came to the basic realization that people will believe those things they want to believe in the face of all logic and evidence, that they will love the man who brings them the untruths they want more

Mets pitcher Tom Seaver (right) looks on as two great pitchers,
Satchel Paige (left) and Dizzy Dean (center) indulge in a little shop talk
during a 1969 encounter. Satch was then a coach for the Atlanta Braves,
while Dean had developed a broadcasting career. *(Wide World)*

than the man who brings them the truths they don't want, that "there's one born every minute." With the use of the midget, General Tom Thumb; the Swedish nightingale, Jenny Lind; and a three-ring circus, he parlayed this information into a series of fortunes. The medicine-show huckster, the wrestling and boxing promoters of recent years, the movie "tub-thumpers" are part of the same heritage of which Barnum is a part. W. C. Fields both popularized and satirized the image in movies like *Poppy*, and Bill Veeck, Jr. brought it to baseball in full flower.

Not that Veeck didn't know and love the game. Born in 1914 to a baseball writer who became President of the Chicago Cubs in 1919, Veeck, Jr. grew up hanging around a ballpark. He sold peanuts, scorecards, and soft drinks; worked as an office boy; and went into baseball as a career when his father died during his sophomore year at Kenyon. In 1940, he was treasurer of the Cubs, and one year later got a chance to put his experience to work when he and Charlie Grimm bougnt the down-and-out Milwaukee Brewers of the American Association. Success there led him to equal success with the Cleveland Indians, the Chicago White Sox, and the St. Louis Browns, a story he and Ed Linn have chronicled most engagingly in the book, *Veeck as in Wreck*. His success, or at least the methods that led to it, got him into trouble with both "the amateur" and the "cost-account" owners, and he was eventually blackballed out of the game.

Veeck's idea of a good baseball operation was a fine club (he never kidded himself that a winning club was not essential) and as much packaging as he could muster. When Veeck owned a club, a customer not only got a ballgame for his ticket, he might also see fireworks, a horse race,

listen to a jazz band, be awarded a cake of ice or a couple of uncaged pigeons, see a wedding, watch a scoreboard explode, look at a clown, or even manage the team. Veeck believed firmly, and correctly, that there were not enough baseball fans available to support most teams. Thus, he went about attracting the tinker, the tailor, the candlestick-maker who didn't know leftfield from third base, and getting them to bring their sisters and their cousins and their aunts. Many of his promotions are standard fare in the ballparks of today.

By 1948, Veeck's stunts had made him so suspect with the "old guard" that he was actually accused of making a travesty of the game when he hired Satchel Paige, the Negro barnstormer, to pitch for him. *The Sporting News* wrote that the act "cast a reflection on the entire scheme of operation in the major leagues." Of course the fact that Paige was a great character and Black was not lost on Veeck's mind, but Veeck also knew that Paige was still a great pitcher. The combination of good baseball and good publicity was completely irresistible to someone of his outlook. There's a matter of philosophy here. To Veeck, baseball is entertainment, first, last, and always. Not that he doesn't love the game, but that he sees it in terms of "packaging" and the "hard sell." There are an awful lot of people in sports who don't feel this way, and although the dollars and cents side of the game has become so important since television, a lot of the older owners do not want to tarnish their image of being "gentlemen jockeys." Such persons, as well as members of the newer "cost-account" breed who see a ballclub as a sort of micro-IBM or Procter & Gamble, feel that Veeck put too much of the Barnum hoopla into the game, cheapening the product as well as selling people a pattern of phoney promotion that bespeaks quick profit but little durability.

Here, I do not care whether Veeck or his critics are right or wrong. The point is that Bill Veeck, Jr. has been associated with Barnum-like promotion, with turning baseball into a product sold by a pitchman such as Purple Panther Juice—and there is little about his techniques, loud and casual dress, and scorn for the conservative that mitigates this. His most famous stunt is utterly illustrative. Having read James Thurber's *You Could Look It Up* in which a midget goes to bat in a major league game, Veeck signed Eddie Gaedel to a contract to bat for the St. Louis Browns. Presenting him to the manager Zack Taylor in a birthday cake which was tapped open by a figure dressed as Sir John Falstaff in honor of the brewing company which sponsored the radio broadcasts, Gaedel was sent to bat for Frank Saucier in the first inning of a meaningless game with the Tigers. Bob Cain walked him, and he trotted down to first where Jimmy Delsing pinch-ran for him. His career was the shortest possible. Nonetheless, Veeck was roundly attacked for executing such an indignity, and Will Harridge, President of the American League, issued an order that banned Gaedel from baseball and stated that all future contracts must be approved by the League Office. Veeck, who knew what the reaction would be and couldn't have cared less, simply justified the whole affair in the fact

Pitching great Rube Waddell shows his championship form. *(Culver Pictures, Inc.)*

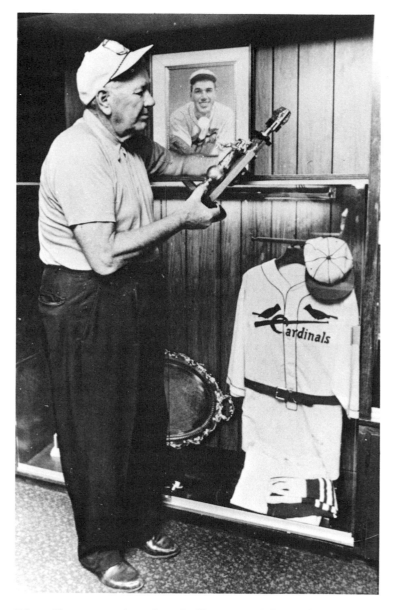

Dizzy Dean examines baseball memorabilia at his home in Wiggins, Mississippi, shortly before his death. *(Wide World)*

that the fans loved it and would come back to the ballpark to see what might happen next. To the "old guard" it was like raping Betsy Ross. To the "cost-account" breed it was "immature" and "a dangerous precedent." As no reconciliation was possible, baseball rusticated Bill Veeck, Jr., perhaps forever—but not without appropriating, in more dignified form, many of his Purple Panther-flavored ideas.

The stereotype of the frontier roarer has always been easy to adapt to the national game where year after year dozens of country boys still damp behind the ears are brought in sudden contact with the city. Rube Waddell, and later Dizzy Dean, serve as archetypes of this recurring figure, their personalities such that the public would gladly believe they once rassled bears, shot pipes from their bunkmate's lips, or never learned to read. In fact, the pictures given of Waddell would fit Mike Fink or Davy Crockett were either of those roarers to don a baseball rather than a coonskin cap.

Waddell first shows up at his big league club, Louisville, at 3:30 in the morning. Wearing, of course, a dinky country cap, general store clothes, and carrying a suitcase with only red ties in it, he rouses his manager-to-be, Fred Clarke, by knocking on the door of the hotel room. His greeting to Clarke is a hearty handshake and a request to borrow two bucks. When Clarke inquires "who the hell" this is, Waddell replies, "Your new man, the world's greatest pitcher!" —a fact the intolerant Clarke never benefitted from. Irrepressibly Waddell then goes from room to room greeting his new teammates and collecting about $16.

Soon his eccentricities, his capacity for liquor, and his feverish sex drive distinguish him from normal humanity and catch the public fancy. No one, not even the managers he drove nuts, could help liking the guy—insouciant and friendly as a pup. Under the tutelage of Connie Mack and with the aid of a series of detectives who followed him everywhere, Waddell did finally emerge as "the world's greatest pitcher," his eccentricities ever-present. So he twirls both ends of a doubleheader, allowing but two runs in 26 innings, and then goes fishing before his teammates can congratulate him; so he pulls in the outfield and strikes out the side; so he rooms with Ossie Schreck who is a near-alcoholic fond of munching animal crackers in bed. One year he threatens to quit baseball for vaudeville and does act in a melodrama called *The Stain of Guilt* in which he takes his role so seriously that he actually beats up the villains on the stage. He puts limburger cheese and onion into the sick-bed of Connie Mack to make him feel better. He dives into the Delaware River in a vain attempt to rescue a man he felt had fallen from a ferry, even though there was no one in the water. He carries a teammate beaned by a pitch out of the ballpark to the street, hails a carriage, and then at the hospital sits up the whole night with his pal's head cradled in his hands. Continually in trouble with the law for non-support, he nonetheless goes out like a hero, contracting tuberculosis in some a-medical fashion from helping to plug a levee in a river flood and dying "less than two years" later with the clear implication that he would "still be alive" if he hadn't been so kind-hearted. This was a walking tall-tale—a man whose deeds needed but the slightest touch here and there to be stranger than any fiction. In fact, Rube Waddell might well be the hero of the modern joke cycles: a Moron, a Hophead, a Kilroy, or a Polack. It would not be hard to see him mistaking an auto accident for a ballgame; going to the ball-park to see "the pitcher's box" and coming home delighted because one got "knocked out"; or hearing the umpire say he has four balls on him and ripping open his trousers to find out if it is really so.

Ole Diz, Dizzy Dean, was cut from pretty much the same cloth, except that by Dean's day there was a career beyond baseball in this image. Where Waddell and King Kelly could turn a few bucks on the vaudeville stage because of their eccentric reputations, Dean had open to him the whole field of endorsement, mass production, radio, and a well-established "rubber chicken circuit." And he capitalized on himself utterly, so much so that there is a ring of commercialism about Dean that never sounds about Waddell. Waddell would have been the country braggart, too ignorant, too careless for polite ways whether there were money in it or not. Dean, in league with his wife Pat, smelled the air and cultivated his natural propensities, shaping them and molding them to fit the mass taste. In brief, Dean was developed as a frontier braggart, but one polite enough for mass production.

Nonetheless, Jay Hanna Dean, he said he borrowed the more widely known Jerome Herman to make the father of a dead boy feel better, was a genuine country bumpkin. Born to share-cropping parents in Lucas, Arkansas, in 1911, Dean had worked in the cotton fields; seen his mother, a sister, and a brother die young; known extreme poverty first-hand; and received almost no education. Trained for a baseball career by a father who used everything from hickory nuts to bits of inner tubes wrapped in shoe-tongues for balls, Dean played his first organized games in the Army at Fort Sam Houston. Eventually buying his way out of the service, he was signed to a St. Louis

Cardinal contract when 18. To hear Dean tell of these days is to hear a series of well-established sub-literary clichés. He eats sowbelly, black-eyed peas, and milk for breakfast. He accounts for his second-grade education by saying, "If I'd a-went to third grade, I'd of passed up my old man." He recalls how he shovelled manure in the army. Asked by an officer when he might bring a load over for a flower bed, he replies innocently, "Right soon, sir, you're number two on my shit-list."

Nor does the pattern change when he enters organized ball. With but one suit of clothes and no knowledge of laundry, he appears at St. Joseph in the Western Association in 1930. He wins his first game 4–3, supposedly asking each batter which sort of pitch he prefers and then, in the old way, throwing whatever is requested. In the same game, he starts a triple play. After hours, he horses around, even ending up in the pokey for racing the police chief through traffic. When called up to Houston, he twirls a 12–1 masterpiece for his debut. Immediately, he drops in to the President's suite to apologize for letting "them bums" get the one run. A few nights later, meeting the same gentleman in the hotel lobby at 2 A.M., he remarks, "Well, I guess you and me will get the devil for this, but I won't say nothing about it if you don't."

After he moves up to the Cardinals, only his eccentric behavior and the inability of Gabby Street to tolerate his insouciance prevent him from making the team. Everytime he pitches he is sensational, filling the bases on purpose and then striking out Al Simmons, Mickey Cochrane, and Jimmy Foxx on ten blinding pitches. Sent back to Houston for seasoning that simply isn't needed, he burns up the Texas League, winning 26 games and a wife who brings stability and practicality into his life—"as a good woman always will." The result is promotion to the Cards in 1932 and the start of a short, but spectacular, major league career.

The funny thing about this cliché-ridden version of Dean's life is that it is essentially accurate, with but a minimum of flavor added. Dean was lucky. He simply had to remain true to his roots to be what people wanted. The only danger was in letting money, success, and expanding horizons change the public image—a danger he initially combatted fairly well. So old Diz named his conservative, colorless brother "Daffy"; announced "Me and Paul" would win 40–45 games in the 1934 season; and requested permission to pitch the entire World Series himself. He put on a blanket and built a bonfire in front of the dugout to warm his hands when the temperature was 100°; put a cake of ice on home plate to cool off his fastball; was photographed roping calves; wore ten-gallon hats and levis. His active mind, synchronized with that of his wife, missed few tricks. The press and even the other players fell in step. When he was skulled by a Burgess Whitehead liner, the headlines proclaimed, "X-rays of Dean's Head Show Nothing." "If Diz ever gets smart," commented Paul Richards, "he's through."

Dean was, perhaps, the first ballplayer who systematically capitalized on his career. With Pat to run the hard-headed side of the show, Dizzy Dean T-shirts, Dizzy Dean caps, Dizzy Dean booklets, "Me and Paul" this-and-that flooded the market. "Me and Paul" toured in vaudeville; there was a radio program, even a comic strip. Eventually Diz sold his life-story to Hollywood where it was made into a trite picture, *The Pride of St. Louis*, starring Dan Dailey. And through the whole affair walked a ghost of American frontier literature—the lovable, careless, amoral bumpkin who somehow found himself in a twentieth-century world.

Unfortunately Dean was a real rustic, not a character in a cycle of pulp literature where the author has complete control. Success spoiled him. Money and fame gave him a grossly swelled head. In 1935 clear signs that he could not remain publicly true to his legendary image began to show. Stories of Dean's crankiness with the press, irritability to his teammates, ill-natured desire to establish his own rules were becoming widely known. Annoyed in Pittsburgh by a bad call that he felt led to a Pirate rally, he quit trying in front of thousands of fans, lobbing the ball to the plate. He got into a fight with his catcher Virgil Davis. Dean thought Davis had failed to hustle on a foul ball in Cincinnati during a 3–2 loss. When his turn came up again, he refused to let Davis catch him, much to his teammates' outspoken disgust. He felt he was underpaid and publicly called Sam Breardon and Branch Rickey cheapskates. It didn't matter that Dean was at least not clearly wrong in his feelings. What mattered was that it undermined the good-nature of the Rube Waddell image. The fans turned against him, his extra-curricular income fell off, he was constantly booed.

But there was too much money involved. By the spring of 1936, when he saw that the attitude which had culminated in a holdout was hurting only Diz, he "reformed"—or rather tried to re-establish the image He treated fans, teammates, and umpires much better; pitched out of turn; worked in the bullpen; didn't follow through with his crabbing. And "the suckers born each minute" began to forgive him, rationalizing that a swelled-head (at least when cured) was part of the characterization after all. In fact, the great irony of the Dean story is that when Earl

Averill broke Dean's toe with a liner in the 1937 All-Star Game, Dizzy's determination to restore his image cost him his pitching career. Instead of resting, he insisted on staying with the Cardinals and what's more pitching. With the aching toe sticking from his shoe, he developed a herky-jerky motion that led to a sore arm and won him but one of seven starts. In 1938, he was traded to the Cubs primarily as a gate-attraction. Though he managed to win 7 and lose but 1 with a fine 1.80 E.R.A. in 75 innings of work, his value as a pitcher was "sporadic" at best.

This rapid denouement had one sentimental climax within it. The Cubs won the pennant in 1938, and they started Dean, who but four years earlier had made the World Series a personal triumph, in the second game against the Yankees. Dean, with no fastball, just savvy, change of pace, and guts did a moving job. He held the well-named Bronx Bombers to one run for 7⅔ innings. Then, with a truly remarkable victory within his grasp he was beaten in the most ironic, yet appropriate, of ways. Frankie Crosetti, a weak-hitting gloveman, came up with two out and a man on first. He hit that "slow pitch you should never throw a weak batter" over the wall. The newsmen went into a sentimental orgy, hurrying out their finest commonplaces: "twilight of his career," "the long walk to the clubhouse," "even Yankee throats a bit tight," "sheer guts," "you knew it was coming, but . ." Although Dean was with the Cubs in 1939, his playing career ended when that fly entered the stands. He retired in 1940, after a hopeless try in the Texas League, another garland withered away.

But Ole Diz had built an image that didn't necessarily have to have an active ballplayer behind it, and by 1941 he was back in the limelight announcing St. Louis Browns games for the Falstaff Brewing Corporation. As a commentator, he found his country image flourishing as never before. He set himself up as "the old ballplayer sitting next to you in the bleachers" and announced baseball as a running projection of his ego, singing "The Wabash Cannonball"; using his country language; criticizing players, managers and umps; often alternating brutal honesty with the tallest of lies. He chatted about his bird dogs, cotton pickin' youth, minor league cronies. He commented on politics, morality, things in general. He drank Falstaff beer and belched on the air. He admitted the re-creation of the road-game by telegraph ticker was a pile of malarky. He used phrases like "he slud into second, but was almost throwed out"; "don't fail to miss tomorrow's game"; "the score's nothin' to nothin', nobody's winning"; "they returned to their respectable bases." He was even able to convince some schoolmarms to object that he was ruining their efforts to teach youngsters decent English. The fans loved it, and Dean was again a success, his ego, as well as his bank account, overflowing.

By 1953, when he was elected to the Baseball Hall of Fame, he was, excepting Babe Ruth, the best known player who ever lived, his name as familiar to Americans as that of Little Orphan Annie. And he did it after but eight years in the majors, during two of which he could hardly pitch, and after twelve years before a mike. Dean hard-sold a product that Americans crave, and when he stated in his acceptance speech at Cooperstown that he wanted to thank the Good Lord "for giving him a good right arm, a strong back, and a weak mind" he paid tribute to the frontier image that had taken him so far.

If one adds a bit of the shrewd Yankee to this frontier roarer and subtracts a bit of braggadocio, he comes up with another standard character in folk and popular literature. These are heroes of stories about "wily beguiled," stories in which Simon simply "takes" the pieman before that entrepreneur can take him. In America such clever coneys are apt to be country fellows or immigrants freshly arrived in the city where they encounter the greedy crooks. A classic situation of this sort was used by O. Henry in a little known tale, "Simmons' Saturday Night." In that story Simmons, who seems to be a rube, plays cards in Houston with some "coneycatchers." The gamblers set him up for the "kill." Finally, when he appears drunk and there is $2200 in the pot, his opponent deals four aces into his own hand and four kings to his "coney." However, as the cards are laid down, Simmons tops the four aces with a queen high, straight-heart flush, brushes the money into a carpet bag, and pulls a pistol, remarking,

Gentlemen . . . I invite you all when in New York to call at my joint, at 2508 Bowery. Ask for Diamond Joe, and you'll see me. I'm going into Mexico for two weeks to see after my mining plants and I'll be home any time after then. Up stairs, 2508 Bowery; don't forget the number. I generally make my travelling expenses as I go. Good night.

Sportswriters are well aware of the Simmons-type hero and from time to time have attempted to fit a player or manager into the formula. Casey Stengel, bandy-legged, wrinkled cast-off, who became one of the most successful managers the Yankees ever had, was a natural for this role. Furthermore, he was willing to cooperate fully. Known throughout his successful, but not unusual, playing career as an eccentric, Stengel always had printable copy for the press, reminding them of the time he tipped his

"The Old Perfesser," Casey Stengel, is surrounded by jubilant Yankees
after the team clinched the 1955 pennant (the Yankees' twenty-first)
against the Boston Red Sox in Fenway Park. *(Wide World)*

New York Mets manager Casey Stengel bows to welcome
St. Louis Cardinals star Stan Musial
to New York Polo Grounds in 1962. *(Wide World)*

cap to the stands so that a bird could fly out; telling how he tried to "drag-bunt" in the narrow confines of a minor league park and "laid the ball down" over the fence; laughing about how he chugged out an inside-the-park homer to give the Giants a 5–4 win over the Yankees in the first game of the 1923 Series.

Stengel was a fine manager, neither great nor poor. Given mediocre material on the Boston Braves and Brooklyn Dodgers, horrendous material on the New York Mets, he accomplished nothing. Given pennant-winning players on the Yankees, he dominated the league. Naturally loquacious, he soon learned that the press and the American public enjoyed him most when he acted the part of the wily veteran who couldn't speak a coherent sentence and yet never forgot a detail, who seemed addle-pated while "all the time" his crafty mind was conceiving astute moves and trepanning his off-guard opponents. Ole Diz had walked right up to the opposing bench and told them he was going to throw "nuthin' except fastballs" and shut them out just the same. Stengel played the fool and spouted nonsense, but used a reserve outfielder so cagily that his opponents took a whole season to learn how to pitch to him, recalled from Coast League days how a batter should work against Gene Bearden and ruined that 20-game winner's career, discovered the glaring weakness in power-hitting Walt Dropo's batting. And the belief went abroad that incoherence was the "hocus-pocus" of a magician. Before long, Stengel was almost never quoted in language any clearer than this, his reply to a 1969 question asked by Frank Brady of Philadelphia's *Evening Bulletin* concerning the possibilities of livening up the ball.

They already lived up the ball. It's too fast for the pitcher, he'd say, and the infielder too and there is a problem if you would like to bunt, which most do. The pitcher is liable to get hurt and the infielder too and I would say you could say there will be more hitting because the ball gets down there faster and it goes through because you can't get there to catch the ball which you would have.

Stengel, naturally quick-witted and dry-humored, was able to do and say exactly what his role demanded of him. Yogi Berra, the Yankee catcher who followed him as manager of the Mets, was not suited for a similar role. Berra too was supposed to act the clown, in his case the apparently stupid *paisano* who could play ball like crazy and what's more call a canny game from behind the plate. Sportswriters and broadcasters stayed up nights combing Joe Miller's jokebook and old vaudeville routines for "skulls" and malapropisms which they could fluff up as "Berraisms." The public was informed that Yogi answered the phone in the middle of the night; when the caller apologized by asking, "Did I wake you?", Berra replied, "No, I was up anyway answering the phone." When the fans gave him a night at the ballpark, his image demanded he step up to the microphone and blurt out, "Thank you for making this night necessary." But as these assembly-line gags rolled forth, stress was also placed on the fact that Berra was one of the most astute students of hitters (and pitchers) ever to squat behind homeplate, that he was natural managerial material, that his homely, elfin features truly hid a gnomic mind. The problem was that Berra, an uncomplicated, likeable, but definitely not witty man, couldn't help out or capitalize on the leads fed him. He had the right build, the right face to be an astute escapée

103

from "The Three Stooges," but he lacked the necessary natural wit. The result was a sort of national misunderstanding, or at least misconception.

The whole thing points up one of the problems associated with hero-making and legend-building. The greatest chronicler in the world cannot make a hero of a figure who can't or won't play his role before the public. You can, as it were, lead the hero to alcohol, but you can't make him drink. Wilmer Mizell, from Vinegar Bend, Arkansas, was supposed to succeed Dizzy Dean as the nation's "country boy" pitcher. He wasn't cut out for it. Nor was Bill Voiselle, who wore 96, the odd-name of his South Carolina hometown, on his uniform. Nor were conservatives like Joe DiMaggio, Mickey Mantle, or Carl Yastrzemski, no matter how brilliant their abilities. Most Negroes, it seems, are not either—a problem which I had best turn to now.

The Negro, because of the discrimination practiced against him in America, poses a special problem as far as legends go. As I write, it has become next to impossible to develop a Negro into a legendary figure that the whole culture will accept the way it has accepted Babe Ruth, Dizzy Dean, or Ty Cobb. Not that there aren't deserving candidates. Willie Mays is perhaps the finest all-around ballplayer who ever lived. With a colorful basket-catch; basestealing, slugging, and hitting ability; the catchword "Say Hey"; and a series of fantastic fielding plays to his credit, he would seem a natural. So would dynamic Jackie Robinson, the crusader, or Maury Wills, a latter-day Ty Cobb. But one simply does not hear the stories, the anecdotes, the legends about these brilliant players that developed about Dean, Cobb, and Ruth.

The answer is not hard to come by either. It is just because they are Black, because they are members of a self-conscious minority group. I remember Carl Rowan's once writing that the Negro could not consider his battle for equality won until people would permit his race the luxury of criminals, fanatics, and militants without judging all Negroes by the trouble-makers. Transferring his idea, which is absolutely correct, to heroism, I think it next to impossible for a Negro to develop along legendary lines in a predominately White society until the battle for equality is fully won. And this is not because the Whites won't accept a Black hero (I know few baseball fans who aren't willing to accept Willie Mays in such a role), it is because the Negroes are too sensitive to let them. Jackie Robinson once wrote a classic description of Black sensitivity in his book *Baseball Has Done It,* telling of a conversation he had in 1954 with an umpire who had known him eight years earlier when he was with Montreal keeping quiet, causing no ripples. In 1949, Robinson was advised by Branch Rickey to stop turning his other cheek and be himself. "From that moment on," says Robinson, "I defended myself against anti-Negro insults with all the force at my command." Five years later, the umpire, sitting next to him on a plane, asked,

What's made you change your attitude, Jackie? I liked you so much better when you were less aggressive.

Robinson's reply is both honest and *en garde:*

I'm not concerned with your liking or disliking me. . . . All I ask is that you respect me as a human being.

He goes on to explain what he means,

I explained that I was proud to be a Negro. I said God had given us certain unique qualities, that we cherish as our heritage just as Englishmen, Frenchmen, Jews, Indians and every other group of common origin cherish theirs. "I am not ashamed of my dark skin," I said. "You and every other white American should understand that we believe our color is an asset. Your dislike of my aggressiveness has no effect on me. I'm after something much more important than your favor or disfavor. You should at least admit that you respect me as a man who stands up for what he believes in. I am not an Uncle Tom. I am in this fight to stay."

Crucial as all this may be for the Black in America today, it nonetheless is a position that makes legendary heroism almost impossible to attain—at least through the White press. For the chronicler has to move with confidence and broad strokes when fashioning a hero, and if he must "take care" not to hurt feelings, not to picture a man in a way that might "cause trouble," he will move too circumspectly, too self-consciously. What, for example, would be the NAACP, the Black militant, the Black press, the White reaction to a story of Willie Mays' indulgence in some animalistic wenching and drinking bout; to a story of how Jackie Robinson or Maury Wills cruelly spiked a second baseman to make him flinch the next time; to a report that Richie Allen had given the boys in the bleachers "the finger"? The social security of the WASP, of the Roman Catholic, perhaps even of the Jew, is such that these actions can be fitted into traditional patterns which will transcend the ignorance, dishonesty, or obscenity of the particular anecdote. Perhaps the Blacks left to themselves could put such accounts in the proper perspective and enjoy them. When the Negro leagues were isolated, legends of Josh Gibson's tape-measure homers and duels with the great pitchers like Satchel Paige and Dizzy Dean had some cur-

Mets fans unfurl banners in honor of Casey Stengel's seventy-fifth birthday at Philadelphia's Connie Mack Stadium prior to a 1965 Mets-Phillies contest. *(Wide World)*

rency, as did yarns of less savory prowess. But how can Blacks in a White world where they are deeply concerned over "being respected" allow the Whites to revel in them? How can a White chronicler in good conscience undertake to foster them? How can anyone be sure they are not going to be badly misinterpreted by a large percentage of the still biased American public?

No, only Satchel Paige, a product of pre-Black awareness days, has been able to attain stature as a legendary figure comparable to Whites such as Ruth and Dean. And

105

Jackie Robinson holds plaque presented to him on the occasion of his induction into baseball's Hall of Fame on July 23, 1962. Robinson, the first player to break the major leagues' color barrier, was the first Black man to be inducted into the Hall of Fame. *(Wide World)*

it is very important to remember two related things about Paige. First, his legend developed at a time when the Negro was openly discriminated against in baseball as well as in everyday life, when Jackie Robinson had yet to break the color line, when a Negro still felt free of guilt were he to capitalize on the stereotypes that nineteenth-century America had created for him. Second, his legend, as he developed it himself and as the sportswriters cultivated it when he finally became "copy," would pose problems were it developed today. The simple, good-natured Negro clown is a characterization that is clearly obnoxious to current Black, and a good many White, readers. And although there are plenty of persons who are not bothered by it, as the continuing popularity of the Harlem Globetrotters attests, it is unlikely that a writer or promoter would set out to utilize this stereotype in 1970. For Satchel Paige is a "Marster and John" Negro, dressed up with a touch of backwoods roaring and out-and-out prowess.

"Marster and John" stories are Southern folktales told by Whites and Blacks alike. They center on the battles of wits that occur between the relatively well-educated plantation gentry and the slaves who have to rely on native cunning and natural wisdom. Typical is the tale in which the marster brags that one of his old slaves is a clairvoyant, can see what is under pots and boxes and the like. A neighbor bets that the old colored man can't guess what he plans to put under a tub. A crowd gathers. The neighbor catches a raccoon and places the tub over it. The slave is called and told to say what is hidden. He hems and haws for awhile, then finally, ruefully scratches his head and remarks, "Ah guess you got this old coon." His owner jubilantly collects.

Actually such stories haven't been discarded in urban

America. Rather, the old coon has simply been replaced by an up-to-date Black who confronts White adversaries, usually Southerners, as equals. Typical is the one of the Northern Negro who is refused service at a Southern gas-station. When the red-necked attendant whips out a pistol and shoots an apple from a near-by tree to frighten the persistent Black, the Negro up-stages him by pulling out his knife and peeling, de-coring, and slicing the apple before it hits the ground. The aghast attendant then hurries over to the car and says, "What will it be, sir, high-test or regular?" And the Black cavalierly replies, "High-test, boy, and don't forget to check the windshield while you're at it!"

The "gas-station, Jackie Robinson" Black, independent, able to handle himself, even a bit hard, is "the man" to be admired and emulated today. There is no place for "This Old Coon" or his equivalents Uncle Tom and Uncle Remus —their nobility, sagacity, and gentleness elbowed aside by the distaste for their subservience. It makes the image that Satchel Paige cultivated seem so out-of-date, so out-of-place today—the legend as antique as the old pitcher who plays in it.

I recall him in Newark, Ohio, after he had made the majors, his all-Black team barnstorming against a group of Whites under pitcher Ned Garver, much in the fashion of the Harlem Globetrotters. Between innings, Paige sat in a rocking chair and sipped from a black bottle. He used all his eccentric pitches, throwing overhand, sidearm, underhand; showed the batters the hesitation pitch, the two-hump blooper, the barber against the chin, the fastballs Long Tom and Little Tom, deliveries which he had supposedly developed in those outlandish areas where baseball is just learned, not taught. He joked and hammed around,

played first base, and even got a hit. It was a minstrel show transferred to the ballfield—a show Paige had acted out a thousand times before and which had kept body and soul together for close to half a century.

Leroy Robert Paige was born sometime between 1899 and 1906 to a gardener and his wife in Mobile, Alabama. His early years were poverty as only the "emancipated" Negro at the turn of the century could know it. He had almost no schooling, and, mixed up with boyhood gangs, was eventually sent to the reformatory at Mount Meigs. When he got out, he took sufficient stock of himself and his future to start throwing baseballs rather than rocks and knives. 6' 3" tall, weighing about 140 or 150 pounds, he was gifted with an amazingly strong and accurate arm which soon made a name for him on the local sandlots. A Pullman porter from Chattanooga spotted him, and he was brought to the attention of Alex Herman who owned the Black Lookouts. Signed for $50 a month, with assurances to his mother that he would not be led back to jail by the sinful world of professional sports, Paige embarked on his career.

He proved to be a remarkable pitcher, but his athletic talent was always shaded by his naturally comic appearance. He learned to capitalize on both. Throwing his fastball by the hitters was basic, but equally important was the "country coon" appearance. With his size-12, triple-A shoes; his skinny, tall build; his extremely long arms and loose-jointed gait; his reedy voice and ability to speak seldom but with real wit when he did, Paige appeared to be something right out of a minstrel show. As Dean would do later, he had only to relax and be himself to multiply the drawing power of his obvious pitching talents.

And Paige, like many people who grow up in poverty, worshipped money, had a knack for acquiring it, but couldn't handle it. His early career is a tedious, now mostly forgotten series of extravaganzas, featuring women, liquor, cars, and ego. He switched from team to team, barnstormed over North America, Central America, and the West Indies, "tired all the time" to use his words, but pitching day in and day out against every conceivable kind of batter. As time went by, he added a repertoire of tricks to the fastball which was one of the best in the history of the game, and as his baseball wisdom accrued so did his sense of the dramatic, the hesitation pitch, Little and Long Tom, and other crowd-pleasers coming into existence. During these and the ensuing years, the prime of his athletic career, Paige probably played in about 2500 games, sometimes pitching five to seven times a week for weeks on end. Advertised as "Satchel Paige, World's Greatest Pitcher, Guaranteed to Strike Out the First 9 Men," he wore a shirt that read "Satchel," worked for anything from $500–$2000 for three innings, grossed as much as $35,000, and traveled as far as 35,000 miles a year.

However, the real market was closed until Branch Rickey and Jackie Robinson broke the color line in 1946 and 1947. Not that Paige was unknown. It was generally conceded among baseball men that a large number of players in the Negro majors could do very well indeed among the Whites, and Josh Gibson, Sol White, Bill Yancey, Terris McDuffie, to name four, were also recognized as unusable stars of their day. In Hollywood in 1934, Paige had the chance to pitch against Dizzy Dean, who was then at the peak of his career and who had won 30 games in the National League during the season. Dean struck out 15 and allowed but one run in 13 innings, but Paige beat him, throwing a shut-out and fanning 17. Dean is said to

have told the press later that Paige was the best pitcher in the business. There are also a host of anecdotes of how he fanned Jimmy Foxx, Rogers Hornsby, Charlie Gehringer, and other big league greats, including Joe DiMaggio. In fact, one of the most frequently told Paige tales centers on a game he pitched in 1935 in Oakland against a team of major and minor league stars, including Joltin' Joe who was to go up to the Yankees the next spring. In that confrontation, Paige, backed by a pick-up club, struck out 15, allowed but three hits, while losing 2–1 in ten innings.

By the time Paige got his shot at the majors, he was well over the hill, his legs weary, his best fastball gone, and his age between 42 and 49. However, he still had enough savvy, gleaned from thousands of innings in the provinces, to get by as a reliever. He won 6, lost 1, and had a 2.47 earned-run average in his first season, 1948; and in 1952 was able to pitch in close to one-third of the St. Louis Browns' games, striking out 91 batters, and hang up a 12–10 won-loss record. That year he made the All-Star team and was generally conceded to be one of the top relief-men around. But if the fastball was nearly gone, if the hesitation pitch was ruled illegal in the majors, and if his age ended his career almost as soon as it started, his sense of the dramatic remained in full splendor.

Aided and abetted by Bill Veeck, Jr. who had seen the drawing power of this already legendary refugee from the "back of beyond," Paige regaled the sportswriters with stories of his early life and barnstorming days. The memoirs he produced for the White public are very close to genuine folktale. Playing the role of the country Negro to the hilt, Paige reconstructed a career out of actuality, handy formulas, and the "This Old Coon" stereotype. First, he refused to say how old he was, content to let people think that he was pitching while collecting social security or that he had forgotten his birthdate "like most those Darkies." When cornered, he would present various dates, saying his draft card read 1906, but 1908 is correct, then changing his mind. Sometimes he would settle for estimating his own age—"between 30 and 70" being one reply. He claimed the name "Satchel" had come from a job as a redcap he long ago held in the Mobile railroad station, although the size of his shoes was frequently offered as an alternate. He called his back muscles and his diaphragm "Number 1" and his arm "Number 2." He invented a game called "Skidoodle" to allow him to exercise without "permanent harm." Scarcely trying, he cultivated a reputation of being "too occupied" to make practices, trains, even games themselves. When confronted, he came up with minstrel stage answers: "My feets told me it was gonna rain, so I didn't think there'd be no game"; "My stomach was nervous"; or the cab driver was paid by the opposing batters "to delay me." When he did show up for a trip, he invariably had one huge bag which contained three or four suits, several pairs of shoes, and enough pills, ointments, and philters to open a hoodoo shop. "I do as I do" was his motto. Commenting on his own face, he once remarked, "We seen some sights, it and I." And those sights allowed him to present himself as an authority on love, dandruff, straw hats, bridge construction, or whatever might come up. His list of six rules for remaining youthful is typical of this part of the image:

1. Avoid fried meats which angry up the blood.
2. If your stomach disputes you, lie down and pacify it with cool thoughts.
3. Keep the juices flowing by jangling around gently as you move.
4. Go very light on the vices, such as carrying on in society. The social ramble ain't restful.
5. Avoid running at all times.
6. Don't look back. Something might be gaining on you.

The sights that produced such sagacities were always appropriate. In 1935, in North Dakota, a Sioux Indian girl takes a shine to the lean pitcher whom her people name Long Rifle in honor of his right arm. Although Satchel rejects her advances, he does go with her to her father's lodge where the redskin keeps a pit of rattlesnakes. True to the stereotype, Satchel starts to leave in a hurry. However, he stops just long enough to pick up the old brave's cure for snakebite. This jug of "snake oil" proves to be good for rubbing the pitching arm, sending "curative sensations vibrating about the muscles" after a tough game. Paige names the powerful medicine "Deer Oil" after the Sioux girl, Dorothy Running-Deer, and refuses to say what it is made of as fellow players guess kerosene, olive oil, wolfbane, and what-not.

Some of the tales are variants of standard anecdotes which we have come across earlier. Paige calls in the outfield, loads the bases on purpose, and strikes out the side. Or he winds up and pretends to throw three Long Toms. On each Josh Gibson, the catcher, merely slaps his hand into the glove, as the umpire yells "Strike One," "Strike Two," "Strike Three," and the batter nods his agreement, remarking, "Ole Satch is so fast today you can hardly see 'em leave his hand!" Others are baseball versions of tall tales known to Negro and White raconteurs throughout the South. The one about the tremendous drive Josh Gibson hit in "Pitchburgh" with one on in the last of the ninth is a fine example. Gibson belts the ball so high and far the "empire" gets tired of waiting for it to come down. In disgust, he finally rules the ball a homer and Paige's team the winner. The next day in Philly, where the same teams are playing again, the ball suddenly comes out of the sky and drops into the centerfielder's glove. The "empire" sees it and shouts at Gibson, "You're out, man. You lose, yestiday in Pitchburgh!"

However, the bulk of the stories are the exaggerated personal adventure. Playing the House of David, Paige throws "the barber" at a bearded hitter and clips his whiskers. The "empire" rules the batter has been hit by the pitch and waves him toward first. Paige protests, stroking the batter's beard and showing the umpire it is not part of a real man but simply air. The "empire," convinced, reverses his decision. Another time, he pitches against the same hairy opponents wearing a false beard, only to have it wave in his face and be torn off by his wind-up. He travels into weird lands like Venezuela, Cuba, and the Dominican Republic under Trujillo, places where the fans are crazy and the customs are strange. In Santa Clara, Cuba, fans chase him about the field when he loses after 24 straight wins. On the same trip, a Spanish-speaking beauty signals her fondness for him by dropping Sen-Sen into his palm. He follows her home, only to have to woo her through a barred window while pigs sleep snoring against his legs. Later, when the family let him enter the house, he realizes too late that this is an indication that the couple are engaged. Satch is able to escape only after a wild ride on a jackass across some mountains and a hasty

motorboat trip out to an American ship steaming opportunely by. In Ciudad Trujillo, brought in with some buddies to win the Winter Series, he pitches with armed soldiers at attention along the baselines, knowing he will never get home alive should he lose. He meets up with savage Indians who run out of the Venezuelan jungle in G-strings to steal baseballs from the players. Later these same natives force him at blow-gun point to eat bugs, roots, and raw pig. He fights bulls in Mexico. He boxes with then lightheavyweight champion John Henry Lewis, raps Lewis on the head, and is knocked cold for his audacity. He fails to recognize Groucho Marx who visits the locker room and cracks a lot of funny jokes. Paige, not appreciating the presence of another humorist, gives the celebrity the cold shoulder, dead-pan treatment and sends him slinking away. Later he claims he didn't recognize Groucho because Marx wasn't wearing fake eyebrows.

Through it all, Paige maintains the role of the simple, uncomplicated Darkie whose country exterior hides a fast-moving, clever mind and whose scarecrow body disguises fantastic pitching ability. To see this figure running down the road at the end of a silent movie, carrying a stolen chicken, pursued by an angry sheriff, would change nothing. And you know, social reform aside, it is a genuine, comic role—as genuine as the *miles gloriosus*, the fop, the music hall Hebe, or the frontier roarer—warm, lovable, laughable, time-tested. And in the long run I know people will see it for what it is—good fun. As Bill Veeck once said, "Satchel Paige is above race and beyond prejudice. He is [like all great comic types] interracial and universal."

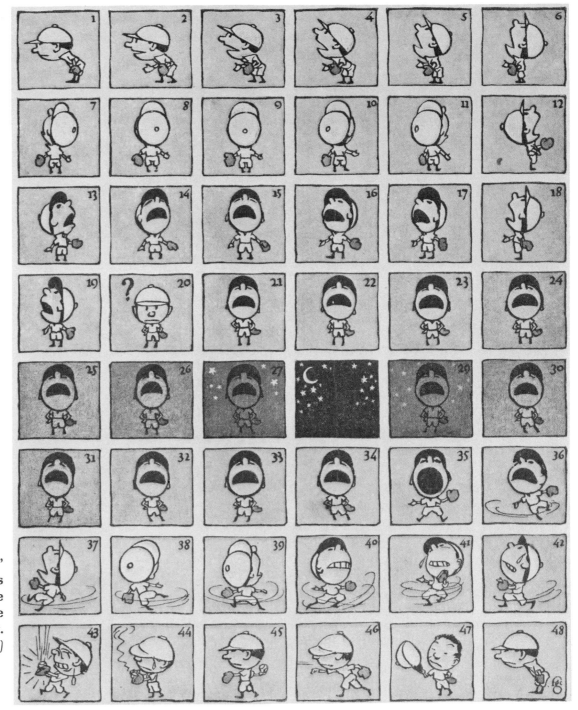

"A High Fly."
Life's 1914 cartoon speaks
volumes about the game
of baseball and the people
who play it.
(New York Public Library)

This illustration accompanied the sheet music
for James M. Goodman's "Baseball Polka,"
a nineteenth-century composition dedicated to "the fraternity."
(New York Public Library)

SIXTH

NEVER-NEVER LAND

RALPH Graber once wrote an article in the *English Journal* on the subject of baseball literature. In it he made the following remark about Ralph Henry Barbour, an early hack writer of baseball stories.

> . . . his clear and vivid accounts of the games in his novels were so superior to the newspaper accounts of actual games that sports reporting became more interesting as his books swept the country and the accounts of imaginary games formed the model for the reporting of real ones.

This is an important observation. We can't just walk away from the legends about Judge Landis, Ole Satch, and the Bambino without recognizing that the "historians" who conceived and propagated those legends had learned from masters—and masters with untrammelled imaginations at that. For where the sportswriter is required by the nature of his profession to foster his accounts from kernels of truth and to anchor his imagination to actual events, there has always swum within his ken a group of authors who have no such restrictions, who can conceive, artificially as it were, whatever they will. These are the pulp writers.

Although not exact, the parallel between the pulp narrative and the *Märchen* is a striking one to a folklorist. As the *Märchen*, or fairy tale, serves the folk community with a body of never-never plots about never-never people, so the pulp narrative gives the readers of the literate society a body of unbelievable stories about unbelievable characters. Such stories serve a different purpose from legends or history, both of which are supposed to have happened. When someone tells you that Johnny Appleseed moved out of a hollow log so that a bear could sleep more restfully or that Babe Herman was hit on the head by a fly ball he was trying to catch, you are supposed to cluck your assent. But when someone tells you how Cinder-sister went to a dance in a pumpkin coach wearing glass slippers or how Frank Merriwell outfoxed Harvard's star hitter with a curve that breaks twice, you are not expected to believe—or, to adapt a Coleridge phrase, you are expected to "suspend your disbelief."

In this never-never literature, the plots seldom vary, relying on set situations of lowly beginnings, cruel reversals, overwhelming odds, industry, and success; of boy meets, loses, gets girl, money, victory; of evil which reigns supreme until goodness suddenly prevails; of untested Davids who defeat veteran Goliaths. The characters, regardless of what people call them, are always named True Blue, Snow White, Coal Black. The settings make no difference: the Western plains, the madding city, the ex-urban home, the ballfield. Give or take a few details, neither do the times nor the medium of communication, that which served for 1890 being easily updated for 1920 or 1970, for radio, movies, or television. And there are signals that tell us when we are about to enter this world. Just as "once upon a time" automatically suspends disbelief for a nursery school audience, so does "Here's to Hudson High, boys" or the "Overture" to Rossini's *The Barber of Seville* for the radio listener.

It would be "long and dry" to trace the evolution of the pulp novel out of the Renaissance novella and the varying forms of the eighteenth-century novel. Suffice it to say that its immediate ancestry lies in the romances of Sir Walter Scott. Scott's novels stress adventure, historical settings, only as much characterization as is necessary, courtly behavior, sexless love, loose plot construction, and happy endings. The pattern, which was easily adapted for American locales by James Fenimore Cooper and William Gilmore Simms, has never gone out of style, being present in cheap fiction, motion picture and television shows, and comic strips even today.

In the years from 1860 to 1920, when its services were extended to movies, radio, and eventually television, the Scott formula bloomed wildly in the dime novel and its more expensive successors. Major links between the dime novel and Scott, Cooper, and Simms were the author Joseph Ingraham and the publisher, Erastus F. Beadle. Ingraham, a real hack, had successfully satisfied the hunger of an increasingly literate population by quite crassly using Cooper and especially Simms as models. His work was reprinted by Beadle and then imitated by Beadle's hired hands like Ingraham's own son, the soldier of fortune Colonel Prentiss Ingraham; and Edward Zane Carroll Judson (Ned Buntline), fabled progenitor of a century of

thrillers. In fact, Ingraham reprints and Ingraham-derived adventures, often focussing on the West, formed a cornerstone of the Beadle and Adams House in the 1870s and '80s.

Also important in the history of the form was Horatio Alger, Jr. Alger, who wrote many dime novels and whose name has become synonymous with the success story, was a Unitarian minister. His novels, deeply rooted in the moist sentimentality of eighteenth-century fiction, are *Märchen*-like accounts in which naïve country boys come to the city and triumph over the social system, cozenage, and complexity by relying on innate conscience, pluck, purity, and a bit of Calvinistic industry. One might call them Unitarian tracts for the masses. But whatever they were, they successfully mingled their sentimental morality with the adventure and courtliness of the Scott-derived thriller to establish a sure-fire formula on which author after author and publisher after publisher could bank.

The spirit in which pulp literature has always existed is best identified by recalling that Erastus Beadle, his brother Irwin, and Robert Adams were all "catchpenny" printers before and even during the time they nurtured the dime novel. That is, they were all at one time or other mixed up in that opportunistic business of chapbook ballads, tracts, and sensationalisms, hawking whatever they felt might be bought for a few pennies by some city gull or country pigeon. They found youth a particularly vulnerable market, and, in fact, aimed so consistently at these eager buyers that dime novels are often thought of as "boys' books" or "juveniles" although many an adult has gulped them down whole.

Typical of the children reading these dream-tales was a

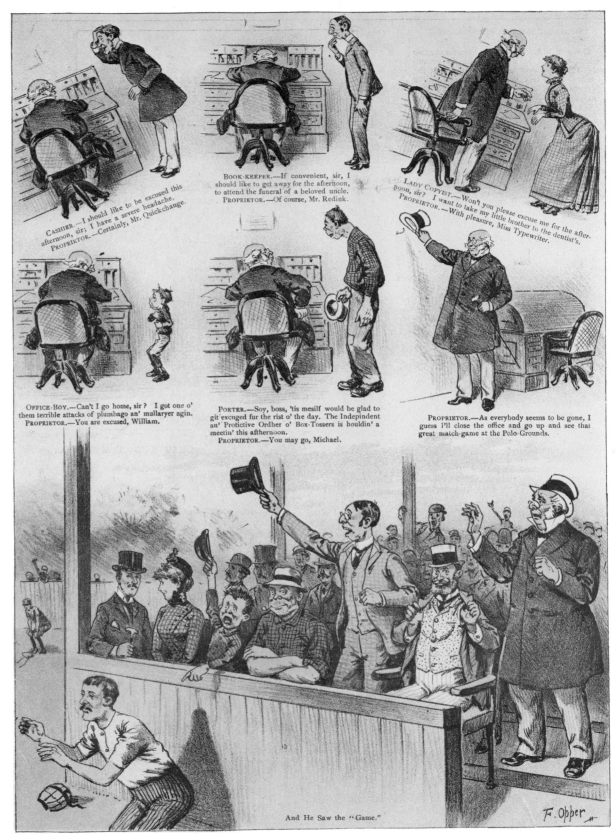

This 1886 Puck cartoon depicts an abashed businessman who meets his entire office staff at a Polo Grounds baseball game after having excused them all from work for sundry reasons. *(New York Public Library)*

Gilbert Patten, creator of the Frank Merriwell stories under the name of Burt L. Standish, centered many of Frank's adventures around baseball contests. *(Wide World)*

lonely, repressed boy named Gilbert William Patten of Corinna, Maine. Born on October 25, 1866, Patten was brought up strictly in a very religious Adventist household. His father, a huge man for his time, 6' 4", 235 pounds, and his ascetic mother did not allow him the normal country childhood, dominated him, and were so fanatically pacifistic they considered even boyish fisticuffs a cardinal sin. Thus squelched, the tall, but skinny, Gilbert William turned dreamer, reading incessantly, particularly the "dime" novels of Colonel Prentiss Ingraham who quickly became his boyhood idol. Eventually, he revolted, much in the fashion of an Ingraham hero, and ran away from home. After work as a machinist, he tried his hand at writing and by 17 had published his first novel for Erastus Beadle. A career was opening, and in 1889 he was even sent to Omaha to pick up enough local color to enable him to write westerns. These he produced, under the name of William West Wilder, *Wyoming Will*. During these years, he had time enough to pursue a lifelong interest in baseball and in 1890 and 1891 managed the team that represented Camden, Maine, in the Knox County League. This was a relatively fast league, and Patten had Bill Carrigan, later a Red Sox star, and Mike Powers, later with the Athletics, under him. In 1891, he went to New York as a professional hack and was to work there for 22 years, first for Beadle and Adams, then for Street and Smith.

It was with Street and Smith in 1896 that he "hit it big" with the Frank Merriwell stories. These stories began in *Tip Top Weekly* written under the pseudonym Burt L. Standish and ran through 208 titles and 125,000,000 copies sold, at times going over the counter at the rate of 135,000 a week. The name Frank Merriwell became a household word and phrases like "a Frank Merriwell finish" conventional speech. Ultimately, a King Features comic strip and a radio program resulted. Even in the twilight of Patten's life, four years before he died in 1945, he published a Frank Merriwell tale, supposedly for adults who had known the hero (or his half-brother Dick and son Frank, Jr.) in earlier days.

The letter that started Patten on the road to fame is reprinted by J. L. Cutler in his definitive work *Gilbert Patten and His Frank Merriwell Saga.*

December 16, 1895.

Gilbert Patten, Esq.
Camden, Maine

Dear Sir: Replying to your favor of December 13, at hand today, we beg to state that the material of which we wrote you in our last letter is intended for a library which we purpose issuing every week; something in the line of the Jack Harkaway stories, Gay Dashleigh series which we are running in Good News and the Island School series, all of which are expressed to you under separate cover, the idea being to issue a library containing a series of stories covering this class of incident, in all of which will appear one prominent character surrounded by suitable satellites. It would be an advantage to the series to have introduced the Dutchman, the Negro, the Irishman, and other dialect that you are familiar with. From what we know of your work, we believe you can give us what we require, and would be pleased to have you write us one of these stories at once. Upon receipt of it, if satisfactory, we shall be prepared to make a contract with you to cover twenty thousand words weekly for this library and a sufficient number of Good News stories to keep them running in the columns of Good News, if you believe you can turn out this amount of work.

It is important that the main character in the series should have a catchy name, such as Dick Lightheart, Jack Harkaway, Gay Dashleigh, Don Kirk, as upon this name will depend the title for the library.

The essential idea of this series is to interest young readers in the career of a young man at a boarding school, preferably a military or a naval academy. The stories should differ from the Jack Harkaways in being American and thoroughly up to date. Our idea is to issue, say twelve stories, each complete in itself, but like the links in a chain, all dealing with life at the academy. By this time the readers will have become sufficiently well acquainted with the hero, and the author will also no doubt have exhausted most of the pranks and escapades that might naturally occur.

After the first twelve numbers, the hero is obliged to leave the academy, or takes it upon himself to leave. It is essential that he should come into a considerable amount of money at this period. When he leaves the academy he takes with him one of the professor's servants, a chum. In fact any of the characters you have introduced and made prominent in the story. A little love element would also not be amiss, though this is not particularly important.

A 1959 New York Times illustration depicted the Casey of Ernest L. Thayer's 1888 poem at the fateful moment when he "fanned." *(© 1959 by The New York Times Company. Reprinted by permission.)*

**A rare chromolithograph,
produced in 1887,
depicting an early Harvard-Yale
diamond contest.**
(New York Public Library)

When the hero is once projected on his travels there is an infinite variety of incidents to choose from. In the Island School Series, published by one of our London connections, you will find scenes of foreign travel, with color. This material you are at liberty to use freely, with our hero as the central character, of course, and up-to-date dialogue.

After we run through twenty or thirty numbers of this, we would bring the hero back and have him go to college—say, Yale University; thence we could take him on his travels again to the South Seas or anywhere.

If you can do the opening stories of school life, you will be able to do them all, as we shall assist you in the matter of local color for the stories of travel.

This letter will, of course, be held as confidential. After you have fully examined the Island School material, kindly return to us.

Yours truly,

Cutler then quotes a passage from the Rockland, Maine, *Courier-Gazette* of January 16, 1932, in which Patten tells how he named the hero.

For my hero I took the given name of Frank to express one of his characteristics—open, on the level, above-board, frank. Merriwell was formed by a combination of two words, Merry—expressive of a jolly high-spirited lad—and well, suggesting abounding physical health. I've never heard of a person, living or dead, whose family name was Merriwell.

Patten has Frank start his career at Fardale Academy and the excitement begins even before he is out of the rail-road station. Alighting from the train, he finds Bart Hodge beating up a young popcorn vendor who has objected to having his poodle kicked. These are the opening lines of *Frank Merriwell's Schooldays:*

"Get out!"
Thump! A shrill howl of pain.
"Stop it! That's my dog!"
"Oh, it is? Then you ought to be kicked too! Take that for your impudence!"
Cuff! A blow from an open hand sent the boyish owner of a whimpering poodle staggering to the ground, while paper bags of popcorn flew from his basket and scattered their snowy contents around.

Frank immediately intervenes, describing the blow as "cowardly." However, Hodge is resistant to reason and must be knocked out with a short right to the jaw, a punch which makes Frank his first enemy.

At Fardale, Frank is popular with all, students and faculty. His charm, athletic prowess, unwavering patriotism, and almost perverted sense of justice are continually put to the test by the machinations of a series of villains and misguided chaps. Nonetheless, he never fails to rise to the occasion: saving Hodge's life and so making that jealous lad his closest friend, winning Confederate fanatic Jack Diamond over to staunch support of the Stars and Stripes, chastening the false pride of bully Bruce Browning. Many of his adventures center on the efforts of a band of thugs to obtain a family ring with a map to a gold mine secretly etched on it; others focus on summer travels in Europe with his eccentric tutor, Professor Scotch.

Matriculation at Yale effects little change on Frank, his buddies, or the stories. New complications do arise from Merriwell's love affairs with two charmers, the dark Inza Burrage (whom he had rescued from a mad dog while at

Methods of pitching: (above) Giving rotary motion to the ball. (Below, left) Straight delivery. (Below, right) The outcurve. *(New York Public Library)*

Fardale and whom he kisses a total of twice) and fair Elsie Bellwood (whom he finally turns over to Bart Hodge). Ultimately, he travels all over the world, becomes an internationally recognized philanthropist, and meets his half-brother, Dick. Dick is persuaded to attend Fardale and Yale where his career is strikingly like that of Frank.

119

Meanwhile, Frank has married Inza and fathered a son, Frank, Jr., who is ready for the Academy and University just about the time Dick leaves. Cutler has remarked that the sum of these "hair-raising exploits make the labors of Hercules and the wandering of Ulysses seem pitifully small and localized." They are certainly no less imaginative.

Patten, who wrote all the Frank Merriwell adventures except for a five-month interlude in 1900 when John H. Whitson produced the tales from outlines Patten gave him, had nothing to do with Frank, Jr., although the hacks assigned to that series used very much the same situations, as Cutler comments, doing little more than "inserting a 'Jr.' in the titles and revising the football and baseball rules."

Baseball is a pretty important part of Merriwell's life and often served as a center around which other excitement might gravitate. I recall a most typical incident from what I suppose was the radio series of 1934. The way I remember it, the "big game" had already started as "we join Frank" tied in the backseat of a car driven by heinous gamblers intent on a betting coup. While the crooks listen to the game on the radio they foolishly cruise around the neighborhood of the ballfield. The final inning comes up, and Frank hears the announcer tell how the opponents have loaded the bases with two out and brought their leading hitter to the plate. A hit will mean the game and the betting coup the gamblers are after. With superhuman effort, Frank works loose from his bonds, leaps from the car, and runs into the ballpark. Even though in street clothes, he rushes to the mound and fires three quick strikes past the hitter. As the fans go wild and his teammates try to congratulate him, he shakes them off and sprints out of the park in pursuit of the villains.

Patten, who also wrote the "Big League Series" about Lefty Locke under the Standish name and the "College Life Series" about Roger Boltwood of Yale under his own name, frequently spent pages describing the sport he loved and knew so thoroughly. In *Frank Merriwell at Yale* there is a classic account. The Blue of Yale and the Crimson of Harvard are engaged in a best of three series between their freshmen teams. Yale has won the first game, but trails by seven runs in the sixth inning of the second contest. Frank Merriwell, barely known to the upperclassmen and spectators watching the important games, is reputed to be good, and there is a certain impatience with the fact he has not been used. After Yale starts a rally, but fails to score, Merriwell takes the mound in the last of the sixth.

So, to the delight of the Harvard crowd, Yale was whitewashed again, and there seemed no show for the New Haven boys to win.

Walter Gordon remained on the bench, and Frank walked down into the box. Then came proof of Merriwell's popularity, for the New Haven spectators arose as one man, wildly waving hats and flags, and gave three cheers and a tiger for Frank.

"That's what kills him!" exclaimed Pierson in disgust. "It is sure to rattle any green man."

"That's right," yawned Collingwood. "It's plain we have wasted our time in coming here to-day."

"It looks that way from the road. Why couldn't the blamed chumps keep still, so he could show what he is made of?"

"It's ten to one he won't be able to find the plate for five minutes. I believe I can see him shaking from here."

The Harvard crowd had never heard of Merriwell, and they regarded him with no little interest as he walked into the box. When the Yale spectators were through cheering Harvard took it up in a derisive way, and it certainly was enough to rattle any fellow with ordinary nerves.

But Frank did not seem to hear all the howling. He paid no attention to cheers of his friends or the jeers of the other party. He seemed in no great hurry. He made sure that every man was in position, felt

A close play at first (left) might easily result in a "kick" (below). *(Culver Pictures)*

of the pitcher's plate with his foot, kicked aside a small pebble, and then took any amount of time in preparing to deliver.

Collingwood began to show some interest. He punched Pierson in the ribs with his elbow and observed:

"Hanged if he acts as if he is badly rattled!"

"That's so. He doesn't seem to be in a hurry," admitted Paul. "He is using his head at the very start, for he is giving himself time to become cool and steady."

"He has Gibson, the best batter on the Harvard team, facing him. Gibson is bound to get a safe hit."

"He is pretty sure to, and that is right."

Merriwell knew that Nort Gibson was the heaviest and surest batter on the Harvard team, but he had been watching the fellow all through the game, trying to "get his alley." He had seen him get a safe hit off a rise, while an outcurve did not fool him at all, as he would bang it if it came over the plate or let it alone when it went outside.

Frank's mind was made up, and he had resolved to give Gibson everything in close to his fingers. Then, if he did hit it, he was not liable to knock it very far.

The first ball Merriwell delivered looked like a pretty one, and Gibson went after it. It was an inshoot, and the batter afterward declared it grazed his knuckles as it passed.

"One strike," called the umpire.

"What's this! what's this!" exclaimed Collingwood, sitting up and rubbing his eyes. "What did he do, anyway?"

"Fooled the batter with a high inshoot," replied Pierson.

"Well, he doesn't seem to be so very rattled after all."

"Can't tell yet. He did all right that time, but Gibson has two more chances. If he gets a drop or an outcurve that is within reach, he will kill it."

Ben Halliday was catching for Yale. Rattleton, the change catcher and first baseman, was laid off with a bad finger. He was rooting with the New Haven gang.

Halliday returned the ball and signaled for a rise, but Merriwell shook his head and took a position that meant that he wished to try the same thing over again. Halliday accepted, and then Frank sent the ball like a shot.

This time it seemed a certain thing that Frank had depended on a high straight ball, and Gibson could not let it pass. He came near

breaking his back trying to start the cover on the ball, but once more he fanned the air.

"Great Jupiter!" gasped Collingwood, who was now aroused. "What did he do then, Pierson?"

"Fooled the fellow on the same thing exactly!" chuckled Paul. "Gibson wasn't looking for two in the same place."

Now the freshman spectators from Yale let themselves out. They couldn't wait for the third strike, but they cheered, blew horns and whistles, and waved flags and hats.

Merriwell had a trick of taking up lots of time in a busy way without pitching the ball while the excitement was too high, and his appearance seemed to indicate that he was totally deaf to all the tumult.

"That's right, Merry, old boy!" yelled an enthusiatic New Haven lad. "Trim his whiskers with them."

"Wind them round his neck, Frank!" cried Harry Rattleton. "You can do it!"

Rattleton had the utmost confidence in his chum, and he had offered to bet that not one of the first three men up would get a safe hit off him. Sport Harris, who was always looking for a chance to risk something, promptly took Harry up, and each placed a "sawbuck" in the hands of Deacon Dunning.

"I am sorry for you, Harris," laughed Rattleton after Gibson had missed the second time, "but he's going to use them all that way."

"Wait, my boy," returned Sport, coolly. "I am inclined to think this man will get a hit yet."

"I'll go you ten to five he doesn't."

"Done!"

They had no time to put up the money, for Merriwell was at work again, and they were eager to watch him.

The very next ball was an out curve, but it was beyond Gibson's reach and he calmly let it pass. Then followed a straight one that was on the level with the top of the batter's head, and Gibson afterward expressed regret that he did not try it. The third one was low and close to Gibson's knees.

Three balls had been called in succession, and the next one settled the matter, for it stood three to two.

"Has he gone to pieces?" anxiously asked Collingwood.

"I don't think so," answered Pierson, "but he has wasted good opportunities trying to pull Gibson. He is in a bad place now."

"You have him in a hole, Gibson," cried a voice. "The next one must be right over, and he can't put it there."

"It looks as if you would win, Rattleton," said Harris in mild disgust. "Merriwell is going to give the batter his base, and so, of course, he will not get a hit."

Harry was nettled, and quick as a flash returned:

"Four balls hits for a go—I mean goes for a hit in this case."

Harris laughed.

"Now I have you sure." he chuckled.

"In your mind, Sport, old boy."

Merriwell seemed to be examining the pitcher's plate, then he looked up like a flash, his eyes seeming to sparkle, and with wonderful quickness delivered the ball.

"It's an outcurve," was the thought which flashed through Gibson's mind as he saw the sphere had been started almost directly at him.

If it was an outcurve it seemed certain to pass over the center of the plate, and it would not do to let it pass. It was speedy, and the batter was forced to make up his mind in a fraction of a second.

He struck at it—and missed!

"Three strikes—batter out!" called the umpire, sharply.

Gibson dropped his stick in a dazed way, muttering:

"Great Scott! it was a straight ball and close to my fingers!"

He might have shouted the words and not been heard, for the Yale rooters were getting in their work for fair. They gave one great roar of delight, and then came the college yell, followed by the freshman cheer. At last they were given an opportunity to use their lungs, after having been comparatively silent for several innings.

When it is Yale's turn to bat, Frank persuades the batter who precedes him, a hapless chap named Blossom, to get hit by Coulter, the Harvard pitcher. Blossom does this. Frank then strides to the plate and works the count to 3 and 0. With a poise well beyond his years, he waits for his pitch, slaps a "daisy cutter" into right field, and moves Blossom over to third. He then signals for a double steal. Blossom is thrown out on the front end, but Frank makes second, and then promptly steals third. The Harvard pitcher is rattled by such daring baserunning. He walks

the next batter, who steals second, and throws the following hitter an easy pitch which is smashed for a double. Two runs come in and Harvard falls apart. When the inning is over the Crimson's seven-run lead is down to three.

Back on the mound, Merriwell continues to hold Harvard in check. In the eighth, he comes up with one man out and a man on second. This time he lines an inside pitch to left.

Then it was that Merriwell seemed to fly around the bases, while the man ahead of him came in and scored. At first the hit had looked like a two-bagger, but there seemed to be a chance of making three out of it as Frank reached second, and the coachers sent him along. He reached third ahead of the ball, and then the Yale crowd on the bleachers did their duty.

"How do you Harvard chaps like Merriwell's style?" yelled a Yale enthusiast as the cheering subsided.

This illustration accompanied an 1896 Harper's short story
about a young boy who made his mark
with his older brother's Princeton ball team. *(Culver Pictures, Inc.)*

When the reliable Danny Griswold singles over second, Harvard's lead is down to a single run. However, even though Frank is able to hold Harvard scoreless in the top of the ninth, steadying the timid Blossom who opens the inning with an error on a grounder to third, it is all in vain. The Crimson hangs on for a one-run win.

Because of his stellar performance in this freshman game, Frank is promoted to the varsity and selected to face the Crimson in an even more crucial tilt. He pitches against a snarling Harvard star named Yedding. Both are in great form and throw shutouts till the sixth, when Harvard picks up a run on an error by the shortstop, a two-base overthrow by the catcher on the subsequent steal, and a fly, the poor catcher dropping the throw home from left-field as the runner crosses the plate. Frank is, however, unflustered by the fact his team has allowed a man to circle the bases on three errors, and the score remains 1–0 going into the last of the ninth.

"Oh, if Yale can score now!" muttered hundreds.

The first man up flied out to center, and the next man was thrown out at first. That seemed to settle it. The spectators were making preparations to leave. The Yale bat-tender, with his face long and doleful, was gathering up the sticks.

What's that? The next man got a safe hit, a single that placed him on first. Then Frank Merriwell was seen carefully selecting a bat.

"Oh, if he were a heavy hitter!" groaned many voices.

Yedding was confident—much too confident. He laughed in Frank's face. He did not think it necessary to watch the man on first closely, and so that man found an opportunity to steal second.

Two strikes and two balls had been called. Then Yedding sent in a swift one to cut the inside corner. Merriwell swung at it.

Crack! Bat and ball met fairly, and away sailed the sphere over the head of the shortstop.

"Run!"

That word was a roar. No need to tell Frank to run. In a moment he was scudding down to first, while the left fielder was going back for the ball which had passed beyond his reach. Frank kept on for second. There was so much noise he could not hear the coachers, but he saw the fielder had not secured the ball. He made third, and the excited coacher sent him home with a furious gesture.

Every man, woman and child was standing. It seemed as if every one was shouting and waving flags, hats, or handkerchiefs. It was a moment of such thrilling, nerve-tingling excitement as is seldom experienced. If Merriwell reached home Yale won; if he failed, the score was tied, for the man in advance had scored.

The fielder had secured the ball, he drove it to the shortstop, and shortstop whirled and sent it whistling home. The catcher was ready to stop Merriwell.

"Slide!"

That word Frank heard above the commotion. He did slide. Forward he scooted in a cloud of dust. The catcher got the ball and put it onto Frank—an instant too late!

A sudden silence.

"Safe home!" rang the voice of the umpire.

Then another roar, louder, wilder, full of unbounded joy! The Yale cheer! The band drowned by all the uproar! The sight of sturdy lads in blue, delirious with delight, hugging a dust-covered youth, lifting him to their shoulders, and bearing him away in triumph. Merriwell had won his own game, and his record was made. It was a glorious finish!

"Never saw anything better," declared Harry. "Frank, you are a wonder!"

"He is that!" declared several others. "Old Yale can't get along without him."

There is a lot of inside baseball in the descriptions of these two games. Frank mixes his pitches; he doesn't just go out there and blow the ball by the batter; he hits behind the runner to advance him; he pulls the "inshoot." In short, melodramatic though the situations and characterizations may be, the games are played and won as baseball is played and won in the actual world.

Such accounts certainly reflect the basic frustrations of Patten's own life. Striding about his study, dictating as much as 20,000 words a week, by this time a colleague and friend of his boyhood idol Ingraham, unable to adjust to his marriages, Patten must have seen in Frank Merriwell, Roger Boltwood, and the rest a dream-answer to deeply embedded feelings of inferiority toward a physically powerful father, a dream-release from abnormal restrictions placed on his animal vitality by an overly concerned mother. His emphasis on baseball also seems to reveal early frustrations as a player, for though he loved the game ardently he was never particularly good at it. Of course, the accounts reflect the basic frustrations of most lives, and obviously the reader as well as the author sees himself in the "Merriwell role." Men like Merriwell are everyman's dream of himself—secure, resourceful, capable; fair, if unrelenting; cool under fire; respected, often eventually loved, by his enemies.

In a government "of the people, by the people, and for the people," any Merriwell will appear a bit fascistic. Certainly, Frank is not "of the people." He is far better than average, with an unerring sense of right and wrong, with a refined ability to evaluate character, analyze situations, and select generally satisfactory solutions. Nor are these solutions accomplished "by the people" around him. He acts alone and in complete command, barking orders at the Blossoms of the world with the spit, polish, and impatience of a Junker colonel. To be sure, all is done "for the people," but not because they request it. Things are done simply because Frank tells the people this is the particular end they have been seeking. The fact of the matter is that Frank Merriwell operates in much the way

that Adolf Hitler and Benito Mussolini once operated, using the basic assumption that the common man knows what he wants, but can only identify it and obtain it through the interpretations of a strong leader—a leader who will take the law into his own hands if need be, who will use violence if that seems the most efficient means to his ends. As the popularity of glorified badmen stories; of Jack London, Mickey Spillane, and Ian Fleming; of Tarzan, The Lone Ranger, and Little Orphan Annie testify, this "I the jury" approach has long appealed to Americans. But it has appealed in fiction where "God's in his Heaven" and "all's right with the world" and where the hero is made to act with an ineffable, Unitarian sense of right and wrong. These same Americans have been terrified to give the reins to the Frank Merriwells of actuality, and thousands of soldiers have been asked to die to protect "the girl next door" from real-life Hitlers and Mussolinis. Perhaps it is all for the best. Perhaps it is by reading about Frank Merriwell and his peers that American Milquetoasts are able to get rid of their urges toward fascism vicariously and so tolerate the more tedious, entangled, but ultimately safer system of Jeffersonian democracy.

Patten was, of course, but one hack involved in providing packaged excitement for Americans through baseball stories. The "Baseball Joe" library written by Edward Stratemeyer under the pseudonym Lester Chadwick was highly successful. The series is not unlike his Rover Boys volumes, written under the name of Arthur M. Winfield, or the Tom Swift saga written for him by Howard Garis as Victor Appleton. And of course Barbour did his share with such titles as *For the Honor of the School* and *Weatherby's Inning*. It may be that Owen Johnson's *The Hummingbird*, published in 1910, is "the best of this early baseball fiction." Johnson, who is still known for his Dink Stover books, is certainly not a writer worth studying in college classes, but he does have a firm sense of plot construction, of the relationship of characterization to that plot, and consequently of motivation. However, to call him "best" is to demand the addition of the phrase "of a bad lot"—a lot that we should not forget included Zane Grey. Grey, who had been an excellent college ballplayer at the University of Pennsylvania and a minor league pro, produced *The Shortstop* in 1909 and *The Redheaded Outfield and Other Stories* in 1915. But he is not remembered for such things. He is remembered for what once seemed an endless stream of cowboy books that sold over 17 million copies in 20 peak years.

Surely without a "bad lot" such as this framing it "Casey at the Bat" could never have scored its steady success. For the defeated Casey, not the triumphant pitcher, is the hero of that wistful poem, and there is refreshment in hearing that "there is no joy in Mudville" and that at least one of these Merriwells of a thousand "hot finishes" actually has struck out. We take the failure to our souls, recalling that day when we were suddenly thrust into the limelight of some Blue-Crimson game, that awful moment when our training, our guts, our luck (most of all, our luck) simply let us down, when groans and slaps of frustration filled our ears—moments we look back on as nadirs to our "Blossom" careers. And I am certain that the year-

This Princeton batter exemplifies the gentleman players who contended on the diamond when baseball was still largely an amateur's sport. *(New York Public Library)*

Hitting fungoes, backing up the left fielder, and catching one on the fly to make the out at the expense of the fielder's dignity are the subjects of these drawings from Walter Camp's Book of College Sports. *(Culver Pictures, Inc.)*

by-year success of "Casey at the Bat" depends on the fact that its audience is unaware that "fate, though fickle, often gives another chance to men" and that "the pitcher" who started all of Casey's "trouble" had to face his victim once more in a sequel called "Casey's Revenge."

CASEY AT THE BAT

It looked extremely rocky for the Mudville nine that day,
The score stood four to six with but an inning left to play.
And so, when Cooney died at first, and Burrows did the same,
A pallor wreathed the features of the patrons of the game.

A straggling few got up to go, leaving there the rest,
With that hope which springs eternal within the human breast.
For they thought if only Casey could get a whack at that,
They'd put up even money with Casey at the bat.

But Flynn preceded Casey, and likewise so did Blake,
And the former was a pudding and the latter was a fake;
So on that stricken multitude a death-like silence sat,
For there seemed but little chance of Casey's getting to the bat.

But Flynn let drive a single to the wonderment of all,
And the much despised Blakey tore the cover off the ball,
And when the dust had lifted and they saw what had occurred,
There was Blakey safe on second, and Flynn a-hugging third.

Then from the gladdened multitude went up a joyous yell,
It bounded from the mountain top and rattled in the dell,
It struck upon the hillside, and rebounded on the flat,
For Casey, mighty Casey, was advancing to the bat.

There was ease in Casey's manner as he stepped into his place,
There was pride in Casey's bearing and a smile on Casey's face,
And when responding to the cheers he lightly doffed his hat,
No stranger in the crowd could doubt, 'twas Casey at the bat.

Ten thousand eyes were on him as he rubbed his hands with dirt,
Five thousand tongues applauded as he wiped them on his shirt;
And while the writhing pitcher ground the ball into his hip—
Defiance gleamed from Casey's eyes—and a sneer curled Casey's lip.

And now the leather-covered sphere came hurtling through the air,
And Casey stood a-watching it in haughty grandeur there;
Close by the sturdy batsman the ball unheeded sped—
"That hain't my style," said Casey—"Strike one," the Umpire said.

From the bleachers black with people there rose a sullen roar,
Like the beating of the storm waves on a stern and distant shore,
"Kill him! kill the Umpire!" shouted some one from the stand—
And it's likely they'd have done it had not Casey raised his hand.

With a smile of Christian charity great Casey's visage shone,
He stilled the rising tumult and he bade the game go on;
He signalled to the pitcher and again the spheroid flew,
But Casey still ignored it and the Umpire said, "Strike two."

"Fraud!" yelled the maddened thousands, and the echo answered "Fraud."
But one scornful look from Casey and the audience was awed;
They saw his face grow stern and cold; they saw his muscles strain,
And they knew that Casey would not let that ball go by again.

The sneer is gone from Casey's lip; his teeth are clenched with hate,
He pounds with cruel violence his bat upon the plate;
And now the pitcher holds the ball, and now he lets it go,
And the air is shattered by the force of Casey's blow.

Oh! somewhere in this favored land the sun is shining bright,
The band is playing somewhere, and somewhere hearts are light.
And somewhere men are laughing, and somewhere children shout;
But there is no joy in Mudville—mighty Casey has "Struck Out."

CASEY'S REVENGE

There were saddened hearts in Mudville, for a week or even more,
There were muttered oaths and curses—every fan in town was sore.
"Just think," said one, "how soft it looked with Casey at the bat!
And then to think he'd go and spring a bush league trick like that."

All his past fame was forgotten; he was now a hopeless "Shine,"
They called him "Strike-Out Casey" from the Mayor down the line,
And as he came to bat each day his bosom heaved a sigh,
While a look of hopeless fury shone in mighty Casey's eye.

The lane is long, someone has said, that never turns again,
And Fate, though fickle, often gives another chance to men.
And Casey smiled—his rugged face no longer wore a frown.
The pitcher who had started all the trouble came to town.

All Mudville had assembled; ten thousand fans had come
To see the twirler who had put big Casey on the bum;
And when he stepped into the box the multitude went wild.
He doffed his cap in proud disdain—but Casey only smiled.

"Play Ball!" the umpire's voice rang out, and then the game began;
But in that throng of thousands there was not a single fan
Who thought that Mudville had a chance; and with the setting sun
Their hopes sank low—the rival team was leading four to one.

The last half of the ninth came round, with no change in the score;
But when the first man up hit safe the crowd began to roar.
The din increased, the echo of ten thousand shouts was heard
When the pitcher hit the second and gave four balls to the third.

Three men on base—nobody out—three runs to tie the game!
A triple meant the highest niche in Mudville's hall of fame!
But here the rally ended and the gloom was deep as night
When the fourth one fouled to catcher and the fifth flew out to right.

A dismal groan in chorus came—a scowl was on each face—
When Casey walked up, bat in hand, and slowly took his place;
His bloodshot eyes in fury gleamed; his teeth were clenched in hate,
He gave his cap a vicious hook and pounded on the plate.

But fame is fleeting as the wind, and glory fades away.
There were no wild and woolly cheers, no glad acclaim this day.
They hissed and groaned and hooted as they clamored, "Strike him
     out,"
But Casey gave no outward sign that he had heard this shout.

The pitcher smiled and cut one loose; across the plate it sped;
Another hiss, another groan—"Strike one!" the umpire said.
Zip! Like a shot, the second curve broke just below his knee—
"Strike two!" the umpire roared aloud; but Casey made no plea.

No roasting for the umpire now—his was an easy lot,
But here the pitcher whirled again—was that a rifle shot?
A whack! A crack! And out through space the leather pellet flew—
A blot against the distant sky, a speck against the blue!

Above the fence in center field, in rapid whirling flight
The sphere sailed on; the blot grew dim and then was lost from sight.
Ten thousand hats were thrown in air, ten thousand threw a fit;
But no one ever found the ball that mighty Casey hit!

Oh, somewhere in this favored land dark clouds may hide the sun,
And somewhere bands no longer play and children have no fun;
And somewhere over blighted lives there hangs a heavy pall;
But Mudville hearts are happy now, for Casey hit the ball!

"Casey's Revenge" puts the whole matter back into the "never-never" world of Frank Merriwell, ruining the poignancy of the original by removing it from life as most of us have to live it. We have done our best to forget that it exists.

Ernest Lawrence Thayer, the author of the two poems, was a well-to-do Harvard graduate who got into the whole business by accident. Son of a prominent Worcester, Massachusetts mill owner, he had majored in philosophy in college, written a Hasty Pudding Club musical, and edited the *Lampoon*. A baseball fan, whose roommate Sam Winslow captained the senior baseball team, he made Phi Beta Kappa and was named Ivy orator of his class. He was in Paris, broadening himself, when another college pal, William Randolph Hearst, cabled him asking if he would write a humor column for the San Francisco *Examiner*. Hearst, who had been thrown out of Harvard for preferring practical jokes and high living to studies, had just begun his newspaper career. His father, George, running for the U.S. Senate, had bought the *Examiner* to promote his candidacy and when he found a drop-out son on his hands he mated the two.

Thayer was willing to turn his collegiate talents to such a column and began writing for the *Examiner* in October 1886. Most of his stuff was unsigned, but in the fall of 1887, he did a series of "ballads" under the by-line

The New York Illustrated News published this whimsical interpretation
of "The Baseball Game of the Future" with the prediction ". . .
the players will have to wear armor to protect their
bodies from the fearful onslaughts." *(Culver Pictures, Inc.)*

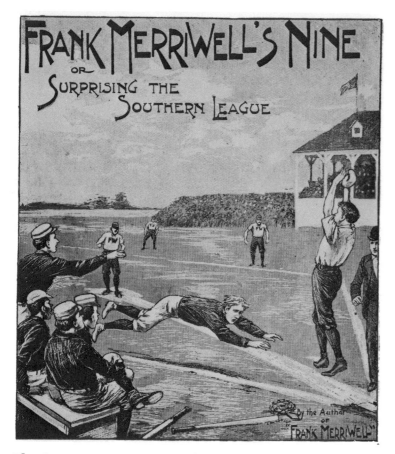

The August 21, 1897 cover of Tip Top Weekly featured an illustration of the climactic moment in "Frank Merriwell's Nine." *(Granger)*

"Phin," an abbreviation of his college nickname, "Phinney." "Casey at the Bat" appeared on Sunday, June 3, 1888, under this signature next to a column by a far better writer, Ambrose Bierce. It was clearly conceived as a sort of "Peanuts-type" poem, a little vignette showing the frus-

trations that come to man. No one paid any attention to it, and it went out of most homes with the garbage. About a month later, Casey got his stereotyped chance to redeem himself.

Both poems would have vanished forever had not pure chance taken over. In New York City a rising young singer and monologuist, William deWolf Hopper, was appearing in a comic opera, *Prince Methusalem,* at Wallach's Theatre, 30th and Broadway. It was "Baseball Night," probably August 14, 1888 (though there is some dispute about the date), and members of the Chicago White Sox and New York Giants were in the audience. Hopper needed a piece to do *entr'act* for these guests. "Casey at the Bat," Thayer's poem which a friend had clipped from the *Examiner,* proved to be the answer, and Hopper memorized it in about an hour and presented it midway in the second act. In his memoirs, sub-titled *Once a Clown, Always a Clown,* Hopper tells how the house "shouted its glee" at the ending. "They had expected," he says, "as anyone does on hearing 'Casey' for the first time, that the mighty batsman would slam the ball out of the lot, and a lesser bard would have had him do so. . . ." Alas, "Casey's Revenge" proves Thayer to be that "lesser bard" after all.

At any rate, unaware of Casey's redemption, pleased with the tremendous success of his performance, Hopper incorporated the poem into his regular repertoire and rode to fame on it. He claimed to have recited it more than 10,000 times, experimenting with gestures and voice tones until he had it perfect. It took, he said, exactly five minutes and forty seconds. Nor did he learn the name of the author until nearly five years after he had begun his recitations. The discovery came in Worcester, where he appeared in a local theatre. After his show, he was invited to meet the author of "Casey at the Bat," which he did, even listening to Thayer give what Hopper later called "the worst delivery of the poem he had ever heard." Thayer seems to have been oblivious to the fact that the poem was well known, felt well above demanding payment for the reprintings, and refused to enter into the wrangles about authorship. He knew he had written it, he had sufficient aesthetic acumen to know it was trash, and he doesn't seem to have cared whether he got credit or not—though his name is completely forgotten in all other contexts today.

Thayer died in 1940; Hopper five years before. However, by then, the poem was famous and there were few literate Americans who had not heard of Mudville. William Lyon Phelps, the sentimental Yale professor, hailed it as a native masterpiece. In *What I Like in Poetry* he wrote that "there is more knowledge of human nature displayed in this poem than in many of the works of the psychiatrist." Magazine hacks, editors, poorly trained teachers began to refer to it as a great bit of "American folklore," though perhaps the only Americans unaware of it are the folk who seldom encounter magazine hacks, editors, or teachers. It was made into a popular song, twice into silent films, twice into Walt Disney cartoons. Hopper recorded it; so did Mel Allen; Jackie Gleason did it on television. William Schuman even composed an opera entitled *The Mighty Casey*, with libretto by Jerome Gury. And every April it is hauled out and dusted off when the season begins anew.

As the poem grew in popularity, various players stepped forward to claim they were the ones to have "shattered" the air by the force of their "blow." One Daniel M. Casey of Silver Spring, Maryland, went to the grave completely convinced that his strikeout as the Phillies dropped one to the Giants in 1887 had inspired the poem. Thayer denied categorically that there was any actual incident on which he had based "Casey at the Bat." The presence of "Casey's Revenge," probably written at the same time though published later, almost surely proves him right. It is only because "Casey's Revenge" is forgotten that we can suspect there really was a Casey. For "Casey at the Bat" is reality, while "Casey at the Bat" plus "Casey's Revenge" is "insubstantial pageant"—"such stuff as dreams are made on."

I have taken the position here that Ernest Thayer wrote both "Casey at the Bat" and "Casey's Revenge," following the lead of Charles Kennedy in *American Ballads, Gay, Naughty, and Nice.* I am aware Grantland Rice and others have been given credit for or claimed "Casey's Revenge." My point stands regardless of authorship.

This 1948 cartoon poked fun at the ballplayers
who became so preoccupied with off-the-field self-promotion
that they neglected their real business—the boys' game.
(© 1948 by The New York Times Company.
Reprinted by permission.)

THE BUSTER

The dime novel stereotype was most important in establishing the point of view of the earliest newspaper reporters, who rapidly learned the profit in recording real players and real ballgames in terms of Frank Merriwell's never-never land. The games were seen as central incidents in the plot of life, the participants were colored and shaded as characters in a drama, and the reporter took the position of benevolent critic. The result was an after-glow of fact-fiction nonsense almost as unlikely, almost as fantastic as anything Frank Merriwell or Baseball Joe had known—a world peopled by flesh and blood ballplayers who literally roll on the ground at each other's jokes; who cry like babies when they lose or are traded; who love Mom, God, the President, dogs, and little kids; who never belch, spit, wench, or drink; who horse around like a bunch of high school valedictorians. This is the world in which the big game is a near-cosmic crisis, where the pressures, the urge for glory, the failures are gargantuan. The dialogue through which the people of this supposed world converse is far less real than anything ever spoken by a maiden who has just kissed a toad and turned him into a prince. The syntax is correct, the usage impeccable, the flow of logic consistent. Four-letter expletives are never used, and both the monotonous 7-letter adjectival participle and its 12-letter noun are as conspicuously absent as they are normally present. It is only because of the existence of this Blue-Crimson world that football coach T. A. D. Jones could stride into a New Haven locker room during the "Roaring Twenties" and unashamedly make his incredible statement, "Gentlemen, you are about to play football for Yale against Harvard. Never in your lives will you do anything so important." Nor is the demand for what one might call "Merriwellerisms" simply an eccentricity of naïver yesteryears. Recently, there have been "hunky-dory" newsmen like the late Arthur Daley of the *Times*, feature-writers for magazines like *Sport*, ghost-writers of "autobiographies" happily titled *Pitch for Glory* or *Nice Guys Finish First*, who offer today's descendants of the dime novel devotee an updated helping of pre-chewed pap.

The fact of the matter is that people don't care to buy the same old world they have to live in. They prefer to pay their "dime" for things as they ought to be. So there is no way the newsman or the ghost can escape some sort of "Merriwellerism." If he cares to make a living he had better offer the package that is marketable. Perhaps Ring Lardner summed it up best at the end of his boxing story, *Champion*. Midge Kelly, the champion, is a sadistic, completely self-centered, cruel crook. The story ends with a

Ring Lardner, who introduced realism into baseball stories and provided an alternative to the then-prevalent dime-novel romanticizations of the ballplayers' life. *(UPI)*

reporter, Joe Morgan, doing a feature on him in the Sunday *News*. He writes up what Wally Adams, Kelly's manager, tells him to write.

"Let's hear what you've got," said Joe, "and then I'll try to fix up something."

So Wallie stepped on the accelerator of his imagination and shot away.

"Just a kid; that's all he is; a regular boy. Get what I mean? Don't know the meanin' o' bad habits. Never tasted liquor in his life and would prob'bly get sick if he smelled it. Clean livin' put him up where he's at. Get what I mean? And modest and unassumin' as a school girl. He's so quiet you wouldn't never know he was round. And he'd go to jail before he'd talk about himself."

Wally goes on to point out that it's "no job at all" to get Midge in shape, " 'cause he's always that way," that Midge

lives in dread he will hurt somebody during a fight, that he loves his wife and "kiddies." Asked if Midge's father is still alive, he replies,

"No, the old man died when he was a kid. But he's got a grand old mother and a kid brother out in Chi. They're the first ones he thinks about after a match, them and his wife and kiddies. And he don't forget to send the old woman a thousand bucks after every bout. He's goin' to buy her a new home as soon as they pay him off for this match."

Wally even goes so far as to state flatly that Midge's brother will be a fighter too.

"They're a fightin' fam'ly and all of 'em honest and straight as a die. Get what I mean? A fella that I can't tell you his name come to Midge in Milwaukee once and wanted him to throw a fight and Midge gave him such a trimmin' in the street that he couldn't go on that night. That's the kind he is. Get what I mean?"

Lardner closes by pointing out that the reporter might have come up with a somewhat different story had he interviewed the men and women Kelly double-crossed, cheated, and discarded on his way up or if he had talked to the mother and crippled brother, victim of Kelly's first knockout, who would never see the interview because they couldn't afford a nickel for a newspaper. The tale ends on this discordant note.

But a story built on their evidence would never have passed the sporting editor.

"Suppose you can prove it," that gentleman would have said. "It wouldn't get us anything but abuse to print it. The people don't want to see him knocked. He's champion."

It was this man, Ring Lardner, more than any other man, who offered the reader an alternative, who brought skepticism and realism into the accounts of baseball and other sports. Lardner is given credit for instituting a second school of sports reporters, the school represented today by newsmen like New York's Red Smith, Los Angeles' Melvin Durslag and Jim Murray, Detroit's Joe Falls; TV muckrackers like Howard Cosell; and the "dugout diarists" like Jim Brosnan of *The Long Season* or "beaver-watching" Jim Bouton of *Ball Four*. Such "tell it like it is" reporters revel in recognizing real ballplayers to be real people, shocking the dear hearts of gentle readers by showing their heroes not only as trustworthy, loyal, thrifty, kind, obedient, but also as knavish, greedy, petty, insubordinate, alcoholic, semi- or fully moronic, and (especially) obscene. Smith even revealed the close contact between his approach and Lardner's by closing his column on a Blue-Crimson football game the Saturday after John Kennedy's assassination with these words,

. . . Work must go on, but there will be other days to shiver in that crepe-gray heap called Yale Bowl, to be light-hearted about a game for children.

The column was printed in the Philadelphia *Inquirer* under the headline, "This Is No Time for Boys' Games," the same catchword Joe Falls used in that Detroit *Free-Press* column quoted in Chapter 1. That cue "a boy's game" echoes directly out of F. Scott Fitzgerald's *New Republic* obituary on Lardner.

. . . During those years when most men of promise achieve an adult education, if only in the school of war, Ring moved in the company of a few dozen illiterates playing a boy's game. A boy's game with no more possibilities in it than a boy could master, a game bounded by walls which kept out novelty or danger, change or adventure. . . .

However deeply Ring might cut into it, his cake had exactly the diameter of Frank Chance's diamond.

The skepticism represented by the Smiths and the Falls has been good for sportswriting. It has forced both reporters and fans to face up to the most elementary facts of life.

Young Yankee star Joe DiMaggio (right), 1937 home run champion, and Babe Ruth (left) meet for the first time at a January 1938 sports banquet. Sportswriter Bill Corum (center) introduced the young slugger to the legendary Ruth. *(Wide World)*

However, there is a good bit of posing in the whole thing, too. It is so "pat" to dismiss baseball or football as "a boy's game," somehow I suppose implying that real estate or politics or Armageddon is "man's work." For actually the sports arena can serve as well as the drawing room, the battlefield, or Bartholomew Fair to show "what man has made of man." And Lardner proved that—if he accomplished nothing else.

Ring Lardner used to say, "I just listen hard." Then he wrote what he heard, sugar-coating it with corny humor, a bitter pill swallowed with delight by the American public. Coming on the scene when what I have called "Merriwellerism" was at the bloom, he introduced the despair and disillusion of the "*fin de siècle*" intellectual to the baseball tale, hating, in terms of Jonathan Swift's remark, not only "people" but "Tom, Dick, and Harry" as well. Of course he was at once misunderstood and mis-read. Even acute literary critics, noting he was a sportswriter, failed to recognize the sociological significance of the pictures he sketched. The critics have learned better, but much of the public remains obtuse. Deceived by the corny humor, dialect, and commonplace settings of his tales, warm minds assume they are reading just another gilder of life, another romantic, like Damon Runyan or Bret Harte, who wants to pat their heads and ruffle their ears. For Lardner truly writes a tale told of, by, and for American idiots. Lardner, the alcoholic Abe North of Fitzgerald's *Tender is the Night*, who replies to Nicole Diver's remark, "I am a woman and my business is to hold things together," by saying, "My business is to tear them apart."

This misanthrope was born in Niles, Michigan, in 1885, the ninth child into a prosperous, upper middle-class family. His early life was materially comfortable and relatively untroubled. A cripple at birth he did wear a metal brace on his leg until he was 11, but nonetheless managed to play high school sports reasonably well. Like many physically mediocre people, he was a chronic fan, obviously getting vicarious rewards from just watching. He also was a talented singer, wrote poetry, and loved the theatre—abilities inherited from and fostered by his mother. However, like many people who grow up in comfortable surroundings, Lardner's motivation and ambition were not well-developed. His father, who suffered heavy financial losses during Ring's last year in high school, wanted both him and his brother to become engineers. At some sacrifice, they were sent to Armour Institute in Chicago in January 1902, but Ring had flunked out by summer. He then knocked about in Niles, doing nothing, working as a bill-collector and bookkeeper, writing music and lyrics for a local minstrel group. In the fall of 1905, he went to work in South Bend, Indiana, reporting for the *Times*. His job was to cover the police blotter and the courts, a role which allowed him ample time to hone his knowledge of baseball watching the afternoon games. In November 1907 he went to Chicago to begin a successful career as sportswriter, baseball correspondent, and columnist on three papers: The *Inter-Ocean*, the *Examiner*, and finally the *Tribune*. With a brief interlude as managing editor of *The Sporting News* and then sports editor of the Boston *American*, he worked on the *Tribune* till after the First World War.

For half a dozen years, Lardner travelled with the Chicago White Sox and the Chicago Cubs as a baseball

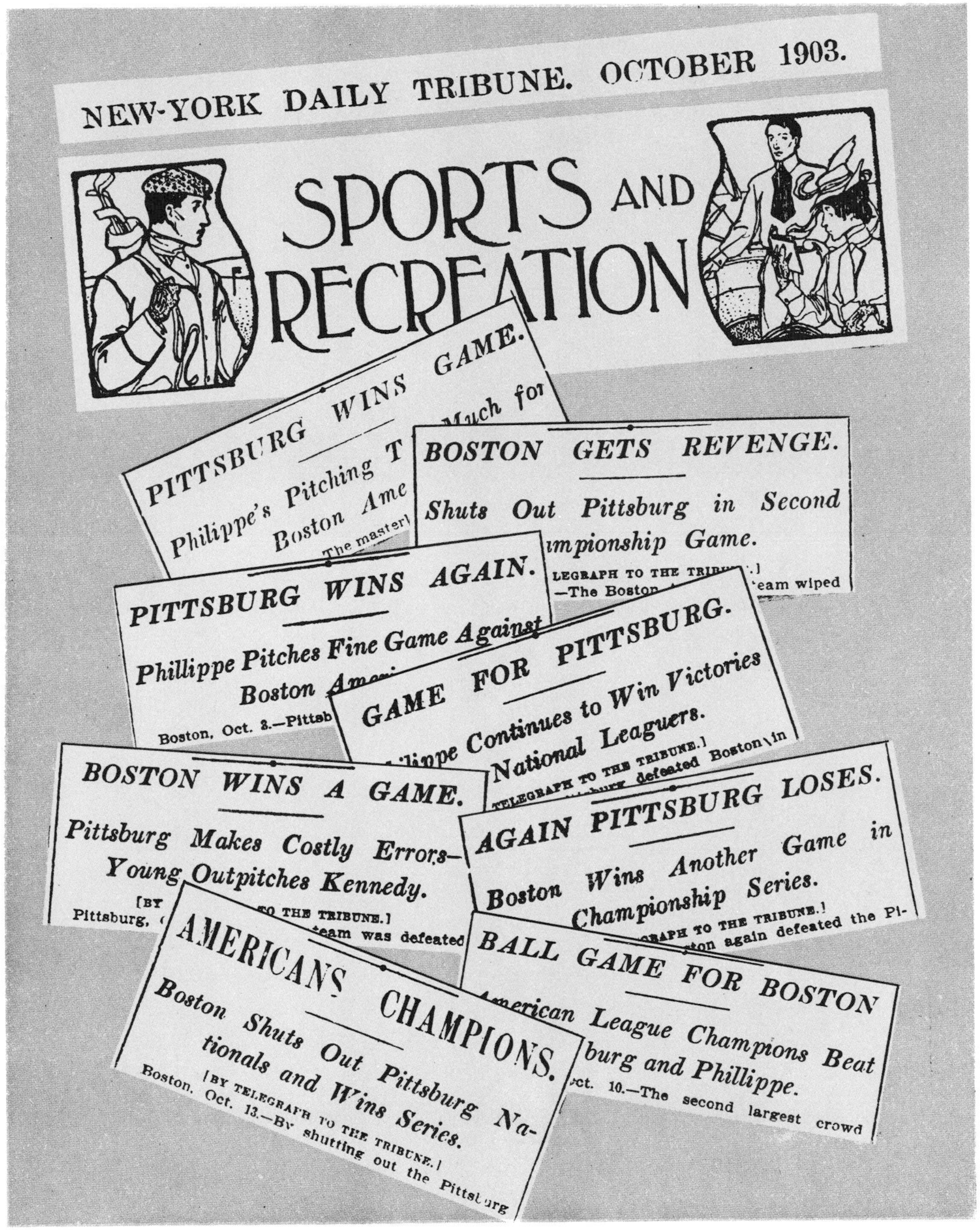

NEW-YORK DAILY TRIBUNE. OCTOBER 1903.

SPORTS AND RECREATION

PITTSBURG WINS GAME.

Much for

Philippe's Pitching T
Boston Ame
The mast

BOSTON GETS REVENGE.

Shuts Out Pittsburg in Second

mpionship Game.

LEGRAPH TO THE TRIBUN
—The Boston

team wiped

PITTSBURG WINS AGAIN.

Phillippe Pitches Fine Game Against

Boston Ame

Boston, Oct. 2.—Pittsb

GAME FOR PITTSBURG.

ilippe Continues to Win Victories

National Leaguers.

TELEGRAPH TO THE TRIBUNE.]

burg defeated Boston in

BOSTON WINS A GAME.

Pittsburg Makes Costly Errors—
Young Outpitches Kennedy.

[BY

Pittsburg, (

O THE TRIBUNE.]

team was defeated

AGAIN PITTSBURG LOSES.

Boston Wins Another Game in

Championship Series.

GRAPH TO THE TRIBUNE.]

ton again defeated the Pi

BALL GAME FOR BOSTON

AMERICANS CHAMPIONS.

Boston Shuts Out Pittsburg Na-
tionals and Wins Series.

[BY TELEGRAPH TO THE TRIBUNE.]

Boston, Oct. 13.—By shutting out the Pittsburg

merican League Champions Beat

burg and Phillippe.

ct. 10.—The second largest crowd

The first modern World Series took place in October, 1903. New York Daily Tribune headlines of the time were remarkably unspectacular in size and tone in comparison with most modern-day Series reports.
(New York Public Library)

139

Douglas Croft played eleven-year-old Lou Gehrig (at left) in Samuel Goldwyn's "The Pride of the Yankees." Gary Cooper starred as the mature Gehrig. *(Culver Pictures)*

Lou Gehrig (Gary Cooper) encourages a critically ill youngster (Gene Collins) in a scene from "The Pride of the Yankees," the Lou Gehrig story. *(Culver Pictures, Inc.)*

140

writer, riding the Pullman cars, playing cards with the players, listening to their thoughts, dreams, and speech. A natural loner, he had developed a professional mask which enabled him to be well-liked without being understood, a part of things without being involved. From a family that could have seen the players and their kin only as people to be employed, Lardner had a detachment toward their speech, their attitudes, their thinking.

"Do you mean you had four pitchers named Kane?" says the big busher.

"No," said Bull. "I mean we had four pitchers that could blow up all of a sudden. It was their hobby. Dave used to work them in turn, the same afternoon; on days when Olds and Carney needed a rest. Each of the four would pitch an innings and a half."

Kane thought quite a while and then said: "But if they was four of them, and they pitched an innings and a half apiece, that's only six innings. Who pitched the other three?"

"Nobody," says Bull. "It was always too dark. By the way, what innings is your favorite? I mean, to blow in?"

"I don't blow," says the sap.

"Then," said Bull, "why was it that fella called you 'Hurry' Kane?"

"It was Lefty Condon called me 'Hurry,'" says the sap. "My last name is Kane, and a hurricane is a big wind."

"Don't a wind blow?" says Bull.

And so on. I swear they kept it up for two hours, Kane trying to explain his nickname and Bull leading him on, and Joe Bonham said that Kane asked him up in the room who that was he had been talking to, and when Joe told him it was Wade, one of the smartest ball players in the league, Hurry said: "Well, then, he must be either stewed or else this is a damn sight dumber league than the one I came from."

Bull and some of the rest of the boys pulled all the old gags on him that's been in baseball since the days when you couldn't get on a club unless you had a walrus mustache. And Kane never disappointed them. They made him go to the club-house after the key to the batter's box; they wrote him mash notes with fake names signed to them and had him spending half his evenings on some corner, waiting to meet gals that never lived; when he held Florida University to two hits in five innings, they sent him telegrams of congratulation from Coolidge and Al Smith, and he showed the telegrams to everybody in the hotel; they had him report at the ball park at six-thirty one morning for a secret "pitchers' conference"; they told him the Ritz was where all the unmarried ball players on the club lived while we were home, and they got him to write and ask for a parlor, bedroom and bath for the whole season. They was nothing he wouldn't fall for till Dave finally tipped him off that he was being kidded, and even then he didn't half believe it.

And he wrote his comedies of these manners with all the cold perspective, all the scornful wit, of a seventeenth-century courtier.

By 1914, just as the First World War began its lesson in disillusion and negativism, Lardner brought forth his first stories in *The Saturday Evening Post*. Six of them form the sequence that was to be published as *You Know Me Al*, once described as "perhaps the most successful dialect narrative since *Huckleberry Finn*." Whether that, or not, it certainly propelled Lardner to the forefront as a magazine writer, opening the road to wealth, fame, and critical acclaim. It did not, it seems, open the road to happiness. From 1914 to his death by heart-attack in 1933, Lardner's life is one of dissatisfaction and trouble, in spite of the continued success of his stories, the luxury of his surroundings, and his contact and collaboration with many of the leading creative people of the time.

He lived at Great Neck, Long Island, part of the "blue lawn, yellow music" world which Fitzgerald, his friend and neighbor, described in *The Great Gatsby* (in fact, Lardner's home was probably the model for Gatsby's West Egg mansion). But although he attended the parties, gave parties himself, belonged to the clubs, and played bridge or golf, he termed the whole thing a "social cesspool." Sick with recurrent tuberculosis, he drank more and more and became deeply pessimistic and introverted. Sherwood Anderson once described him as ". . . a long, solemn-faced man. The face was a mask. You kept wondering . . . what is going on back there?", and Fitzgerald recalling the years on Long Island wrote, "At no time did I feel that I had known him enough, or that anyone knew him . . ." During

The pitcher toes the rubber and peers in for the sign in this ballpark panorama from Twentieth Century–Fox's "It Happens Every Spring." *(Culver Pictures, Inc.)*

this period, he came to hate his dialect stories, actually destroying his manuscripts of them, and even to dislike sports, which had been so good to him and which were to provide his oldest son John with a living.

Of course Lardner's reputation does not rest on his baseball tales alone, although they form an embryo out of which all his work grew. His best stories, ones like "The Golden Honeymoon," "Ex Parte," "Haircut," and "Some Like Them Cold," seem to have nothing to do with the game. Yet they do; for the heroes and heroines of Lardner's best work are simply the sweethearts, in-laws, aunts, and pals of the kind of Americans who become ballplayers. And the world they know, a meaningless world of money games, love games, one-upmanship, and ego, is as well displayed on the diamond as it is in the boarding-house, the railroad station, or the barber-shop. In fact Jack Keefe, the busher of *You Know Me Al*, is but an archetype.

There must be something magical in the bringing together of the New York Giants and the Chicago White Sox. In 1888, when the two teams attended the theatre on 30th and Broadway, deWolf Hopper was prompted to learn "Casey at the Bat." On March 7, 1914, the day they returned from their Far Eastern tour, the *Post* issued the first of "A Busher's Letters Home." From then until the eve of the Black Sox scandal in the fall of 1919, Lardner wrote tales for the *Post* about Jack Keefe. I will not discuss all these tales, which were eventually published as five separate books. Lardner takes Keefe a long way, from his first "cup of coffee" with the White Sox to that point in his career when "unconditional release" is impending. In between, the pudgy pitcher is bobbled about through courtship, marriage, fatherhood; an international tour with the Sox and Giants; the army and its trenches "over there"; attempts to make a living outside the game; return to baseball; degeneration into a heavy drinker with marital problems; and final sale to the lowly Athletics—always just another player with no future beyond the sport, a vainglorious, pitiable gull. Taken as a group, the stories are good reading, perhaps not great literature, but at least at their best, the *You Know Me Al* portion, growing in stature as time goes by.

Lardner had tried his hand at letters supposedly written by athletes when he had the "In the Wake of the News" column during his Chicago newspaper days. Perhaps unconsciously he began to use these *essais* as a means of rebelling against the well-established custom of dispensing poorly spelled, cracker-barrel philosophy out of well-adjusted, small-town brains. At any rate, the ungrammatical epistles of Jack Keefe to Al Blanchard, his hometown buddy in Bedford, Indiana, include no traditional "country insights." In the spirit of *Tilbury Town* and *The Spoon River Anthology* they show a maladjusted bumpkin with about the same perspective that one is likely to encounter in a real Indiana rube.

For the story of Keefe is the story of real talent first marred and then destroyed by real foibles. "*Miles gloriosus* from the provinces" to be sure, Jack Keefe is also a big-time athlete, with a big-time athlete's determination. Although he gets badly shelled in his first major league appearance, although he makes it clear that training rules, advice, practice are not for him, he has enough stuff to come back from being farmed out and to develop into a pretty fair pitcher. Like so many of his peers, he has that cocky confidence and touchy ego, that near-sick compulsion

Jimmy Piersall was portrayed by Tony Perkins in the 1956 movie "Fear Strikes Out." Piersall's autobiography, written with Al Hirshberg, was published in 1955. *(Culver Pictures)*

An 1885 advertisement for Spalding Junior Size baseballs. A price list for Spalding bats appears on the side of the box. *(Culver Pictures, Inc.)*

Nonetheless, unromanticized as the Keefe sketches are, in them Lardner remained true to one aspect of the cracker-barrel tradition. The narrative is unrelentingly moral. Over and over, the incidents illustrate that man must follow the golden clichés: to thine own self be true, do unto others, honor thy wife, thy family, thy leaders, thy word. Keefe, who is an incessant hypocrite, professing "that old-time" morality and practicing almost none, is made to suffer a hell on earth for his sins. In *You Know Me Al* there speaks a chorus—a series of voices that warn the country gull what he is and where he is heading. These "goodly angels" take the form of the other ballplayers, Coach Kid Gleason, and Manager Callahan. Their revelations, delivered in the kidding to which Keefe is continually subjected, are chanted to deaf ears. "Manager Callahan is a funny guy," he complains, "and I don't understand him sometimes." His reaction to such confusion is to threaten to punch "the angel" involved in the nose. The last paragraphs of his letter dated San Francisco, California, March 25 are typical.

Well Al I done my first pitching of the year this P.M. and I guess I showed them that I was in just as good a shape as some of them birds that has been working a month. I worked 4 innings against my old team the San Francisco Club and I give them nothing but fast ones but they sure was fast ones and you could hear them zip. Charlie O'Leary was trying to get out of the way of one of them and it hit his bat and went over first base for a base hit but at that Fournier would of eat it up if it had been Chase playing first base instead of Fournier.

That was the only hit they got off me and they ought to of been ashamed to of tooken that one. But Gleason don't appresiate my work and him and I allmost come to blows at supper. I was pretty hungry and I ordered some stake and some eggs and some pie and some ice

to win, that inability to conceive the possibility of defeat, which allows him to see adversity in terms of poor umpiring, poor luck, poor support, and so recover from it. On the other hand, his utter lack of self-control, perception, patience, moral courage, honesty, or loyalty to anyone other than himself keeps him from being the newspaper sage or even the dime novel Frank Merriwell, revealing him a glamor-stripped Waddell, a fool haunted by compulsions to self-frustration and self-destruction.

cream and some coffee and a glass of milk but Gleason would not let me have the pie or the milk and would not let me eat more than ½ the stake. And it is a wonder I did not bust him and tell him to mind his own business. I says What right have you got to tell me what to eat? And he says You don't need nobody to tell you what to eat you need somebody to keep you from floundering yourself. I says Why can't I eat what I want to when I have worked good?

He says Who told you you worked good and I says I did not need nobody to tell me. I know I worked good because they could not do nothing with me. He says Well it is a good thing for you that they did not start bunting because if you had of went to stoop over to pick up the ball you would of busted wide open. I says Why? and he says because you are hog fat and if you don't let up on the stable and fancy groceries we will have to pay 2 fairs to get you back to Chi. I I don't remember now what I says to him but I says something you can bet on that. You know me Al.

In reading *You Know Me Al* (and the sequels) one keeps hoping that somehow, some way, the kidding may "get to" Keefe and give him a route for escape from his predictable fate. But any such hopes are dashed as the personality of his wife, Florrie, emerges. Florrie forces him to live beyond his means, allows her sister and left-handed brother-in-law, Allen, to sponge off him, insists on a servant to do her housekeeping. She is a savage, unrelenting portrait of the American predatory female who was also featured in such tales as "Who Dealt?" and "Ex Parte." More subtle than her husband, penny-wiser, she ultimately shows herself to be equally foolish as she leads them down a primrose path to emotional and financial bankruptcy and reveals a callous lack of concern for the left-handed baby whom she names Allen and whom Keefe naïvely loves. Her role is to make the reader feel pity for Keefe, who like most human beings is thwarted by a combination of personal inadequacy and chance.

Lardner wrote many other baseball stories. There are five which are still widely read, in addition to the now almost forgotten epistolary novel-length series called *Lose With a Smile. Harmony, Hurry Kane,* and *Alibi Ike* are simply reports on colorful ballplayers, the first about a player whose only interest is singing; the second about a stereotyped bumpkin and braggart with a truly great arm; the last about a fellow who can't face the simplest of situations without making up an excuse or a fanciful explanation. Today it is hard to see them as fresh, they are so similar in tone to the feature articles pumped out by so many of our sportswriters in their endless search behind the headlines. But in the days of Kaiser Bill and Armentiers, they were revolutionary, about to become archetypes.

Possibly no story illustrates the close relationship between Lardner's fiction and journalism better than "Horseshoes." It is about a marginal ballplayer with the Athletics, Dick Grimes, whose hate for boyhood rival Speed Parker literally compels him to become a World Series hero, and is presented in the form of a dining-car conversation between a reporter and the player a few days after the final game. The "inside story" of the recent Series proves to be this. Parker has risen to stardom with the Cubs through incredible luck, yet he has hung the irritating nickname "Horseshoes" on substitute outfielder Grimes. During the season he manages to steal Grimes' girl—a fact Grimes learns just before the seventh game of the Series. Crazy with anger, Grimes gets his revenge when he robs Parker of his bid for a Series-winning hit and smashes an inside-the-park homer in a frenetic attempt to get to third where he can spike his old tormentor. Snidely congratulated by Parker after the game by being called "Horseshoes," he pummels his rival into the hospital and wins back the girl.

Lardner belittled his own work because of its journalistic qualities. What he failed to realize is that all writers are basically journalists. What the better ones do is rise above the specifics about which they are writing and see matters in the perspective of all human behavior. The baseball world, though terribly patterned and trite, is really no more limiting to the imaginative writer than the humour-dominated world of Ben Jonson, the court-oriented world of George Etheredge, or the drawing-room world of Oscar Wilde. Greatness in writing comes not from starting with wide arenas, but from seeing the arena you start with broadly. "To record the parochial in catholic terms" is an apt description of what great writers must do. Virginia Woolf recognized this in connection with Lardner. An admirer of his baseball writing, in spite of the fact that she "didn't know from left-field," Miss Woolf pointed out in an essay entitled "American Fiction" that "games gave him what society gives his English brother"—that is, a meeting-place for the diverse activities of people, a center on which he could focus his observations about the human comedy.

And I think it is in terms of the comedy of manners that Lardner's work can best be appraised. Like some Restoration wit, Lardner was the detached observer of the manners of a narrow world, related though that world might be to folksy American sketches. He made the dugout and "the flats called home" his society, holding the foibles of the inhabitants up for ridicule. Like so many other comedy of manners writers, he was unforgivingly cruel, disgusted by "everyman's" inability to detach himself and evaluate himself. I am certain that Lardner's ultimate rejection of his life and his own writing resulted from his hopeless conviction that all societies, whether of the dugout, the flat, or West Egg, Long Island, are inhabited by fools who don't see themselves as they are, can't change themselves, and won't even laugh at their own whimsies. And this despair, when it begins to show itself in pieces like "My Roomy," is what adds another dimension to Lardner's journalism. As one looks at "My Roomy," he begins to realize how much potential Lardner really did waste in 20 years of pulp success.

The story, written in 1914 near the dawn of Lardner's career, is a remarkable bit of "journalism." Like *Hurry Kane* and *Alibi Ike*, it deals with an eccentric ballplayer, a fellow named Buster Elliott who can hit anything, but cannot field, take orders, or adjust to other people. His eccentricities, such as shaving in the middle of the night, running the tub while he sleeps so it will sound like the dam near home, wearing the same shirt until someone throws it away, are so arbitrary that none of the players can stand rooming with him for more than a couple of days. Unreliable, he costs the team games. Once he goes up to pinch hit and simply lets the ball go by for a third strike, coming back to the bench smiling, unashamed. When the manager, choked with rage, asks him why he didn't "bust it," he offers no excuse but "I was afraid I'd kill somebody," laughing and saying he was "thinkin' of a nickel show he'd seen in Cincinnati." Self-confident in the country braggart tradition, he announces, "They's nothin' I can't do," and proceeds to make a fool of himself at poker. Violent, he beats up persons who cross him. Unlike Keefe or Hurry Kane, Elliott cannot make even the preliminary concessions to the world of reality. And so he fails. He is dropped from the team for deliberately losing a game, his girl deserts him for a soda-jerk, and the players symbolically bar him from their poker gatherings for life. When he finally admits his own frustration, when he realizes that without adjusting he can't get the Series money that will supposedly enable him to marry his girl, he sits down on the bed and begins to cry. His roommate suddenly feels compassion.

He had a kind o' crazy look in his eyes; so when he starts up to the room I follows him.

"What are you goin' to do now?" I says.

"I'm goin' to sell this ticket to Atlanta," he says, "and go back to Muskegon, where I belong."

"I'll help you pack," I says.

"No," says the bug. "I come into this league with this suit o' clothes and a collar. They can have the rest of it." Then he sits down on the bed and begins to cry like a baby. "No series dough for me," he blubbers, "and no weddin' bells! My girl'll die when she hears about it!"

Of course that made me feel kind o' rotten, and I says:

"Brace up, boy! The best thing you can do is go to Atlanta and try hard. You'll be up here again next year."

"You can't tell me where to go!" he says, and he wasn't cryin' no more. "I'll go where I please—and I'm li'ble to take you with me."

I didn't want no argument, so I kep' still. Pretty soon he goes up to the lookin'-glass and stares at himself for five minutes. Then, all of a sudden, he hauls off and takes a wallop at his reflection in the glass. Naturally he smashed the glass all to pieces and he cut his hand somethin' awful.

Without lookin' at it he come over to me and says: "Well, good-by, sport!"—and holds out his other hand to shake. When I starts to shake with him he smears his bloody hand all over my map. Then he laughed like a wild man and run out o' the room and out o' the hotel.

He ends up in an asylum.

The story of Buster Elliott represents a far deeper look

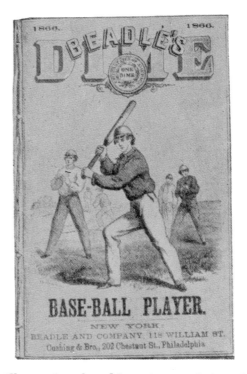

The cover illustration for this 1866 baseball guide makes clear how closely baseball was related to cricket in its early years. Note the shape of the bat. (*Culver Pictures, Inc.*)

at humanity than any "Horseshoes" interview or subsequent Red Smith column. It goes beyond recording what things are really like to investigating consequences, even probing the area of psychological abnormality. The tale may well be an unconscious accounting of Ring Lardner's own skirmishes with the world. Elliott, echoing those words which Fitzgerald put into the mouth of Abe North, tells

148

his roomy "that's my business—bustin' things." And his tragedy, like Lardner's and North's, is that the world neither understands nor tolerates this. Lardner no doubt saw his *Saturday Evening Post* readers as persons not unlike the narrator of "My Roomy," everyday souls who look upon "busters" as some sort of weird "bugs" to be laughed at up to a point, then to be "barred" and dismissed, even destroyed if they get too much in the way. There is no place in this world for "busters" he tells us, except in asylums where they can indulge in their unreality without disturbing normal folks—or in alcohol, where, like Abe North or himself, they can create their own isolation.

Had Lardner begun to probe his despair in 1914, moving not necessarily away from the ballfield, but moving away from unromanticized journalism toward studies of frustration and psychological tragedy, had he developed new narrative techniques, he might have become one of our very best writers. The themes are all there, latent. Time and time again he shows the ability to be more concerned with causes and consequences than with occurrences. He "just never put it all together," as the ballplayers would say. Paid by the magazines and newspapers, always writing commercially, he stayed close to the surface. Perhaps, Lardner's evaluation of himself as a journalist confined him to the limits of journalism. Perhaps, as Fitzgerald says in the obituary, he "fell short of the achievement he was capable of, and this because of a cynical attitude toward his work."

But if such was his fate, it was also his fate to be the prince whose magic act freed the other journalists and hacks from their prison in never-never land and who marked the trail of sports reporting and sports literature along which authors still hurry. For when Buster Elliott broke that mirror way back in 1914, baseball writing was transformed, qualified by the buffet to aspire toward art.

(Clockwise, from upper left) These early illustrations from The Base Ball Player's Pocket Companion, entitled "The Thrower," "The Base Tender," "The Striker" and "The Catcher," from the days of cricket-style uniforms, pre-date the innovation of resin-bag bases. A thin bat was used, and posts served as bases. *(Culver Pictures, Inc.)*

White Sox fans perch on every available ledge as an overflow crowd
of 55,555 watches the home team split a 1973 early-season doubleheader
with the Minnesota Twins in Chicago's Comiskey Park. *(Wide World)*

EIGHTH

A CUSTOM OF OUR CLAN

On the final Sunday of the 1966 season, Sandy Koufax won the second game of a doubleheader in Philadelphia and with it a hot pennant race for the Dodgers. This was the last game he ever pitched in Philly, and it ended after dark. As the fans hurried out across the floodlit field, two professors from the University of Pennsylvania stopped near the mound where moments before Koufax was struggling to triumph. One of them toed the slab and looking up at the obscure stands remarked, "If I had that guy's left arm, damn if I'd be teaching economics." I have not forgotten that wistful comment, and I won't, because it phrases the frustration of hundreds of thousands of American males— Irishman or Negro, Wasp or Jew; that father who shoved the glove into his first son's crib, that unhappy boy who grew up in Corinna, Maine, that misanthrope from Niles, Michigan.

For the "frustrated ballplayer" is an American type as surely as the cowboy, the movie starlet, or the man in the grey-flannel suit. Why he exists is a complex problem. Perhaps it is all part of the industrial revolution, the emasculation of the "male animal," the dominance of women in twentieth-century life. Perhaps it is a kind of "Huckleberry Finn" urge to remain young forever, to escape from "village mores" and Sunday School laws into the atavistic, dog vs. dog world of games. More specifically, it may be related to the discouragement of that moment described by James Farrell in *Father and Son* when a Danny O'Neill admits that God has not given him the equipment necessary to realize his dreams—

For three years he had daydreamed of how he would be a scintillating high-school baseball star and how he would hit a home run with the bases full. And look at the way he had folded up in a pinch. Yes, after kidding himself about his destiny, and having the nerve to think that he would be a star like Ty Cobb or Eddie Collins, he was a miserable failure. Whenever he was in a tight situation, he was a bust, a flat tire. He didn't have what it takes. He was eighteen years old, and he was no good. He lacked something—nerve, confidence. In a pinch, it was always the same. He lost his confidence, When he didn't have time, a few seconds in which to think, it was different That was why he was better in football and basketball than he was in baseball. In baseball when you batted, there were those few seconds and fractions of a second between pitches, when your mind undid you. In football and basketball, you didn't have the time to think as you did in baseball. That made the difference. And it was in just that period of a few important seconds that he was no good. Yes, even though he was considered one of the best athletes in school, he was never really going to be any good.

—to that moment when a man must adjust to the fact that he was not cast to play Prince Hamlet, but only, in T. S. Eliot's words, "to swell a progress." It may even be tied to

Eight-year-old Sandy Koufax takes his licks during batting practice.
Southpaw Koufax went on to make his mark on the mound, not in the
batter's cage, winning 27 games for the Los Angeles Dodgers
in 1966 and consistently displaying extraordinary talent. *(Wide World)*

middle-class ideas of what is "a fitting life's work" and what is not. Athletics as a profession has long carried both a social and an intellectual stigma for prosperous families who would have their sons make their way with their minds or their industry and not with their bodies. Generation after generation, professional sports lose hundreds of strapping lads for no reason other than this, while urban offices win a host of hearts vaguely haunted by a wish to see their names embossed upon bubble-gum cards as well as upon frosty doors.

Many of our best authors have treasured this nostalgia in corners of their own hearts, and true to their duty recorded it along with the "few days" and "full troubles" lived by men born of woman. Thomas Wolfe is one. On January 30, 1938, Wolfe went to the 15th Annual Dinner of the New York Chapter of the Baseball Writers Association of America with sportswriter Arthur Mann. Just over two weeks later, he wrote Mann a "thank you" note that read in part as follows,

. . . I think I may have told you that one reason I have always loved baseball so much is that it has been not merely "the great national game," but really a part of the whole weather of our lives, of the thing that is our own, of the whole fabric, the million memories of America. For example, in the memory of almost every one of us, is there anything that can evoke spring—the first fine days of April— better than the sound of the ball smacking into the pocket of the big mitt, the sound of the bat as it hits the horse hide: for me, at any rate, and I am being literal and not rhetorical—almost everything I know about spring is in it—the first leaf, the jonquil, the maple tree, the smell of grass upon your hands and knees, the coming into flower of April. And is there anything that can tell more about an American summer than, say, the smell of the wooden bleachers in a small town baseball park, that resinous, sultry and exciting smell of old dry wood.

Well, I could go on indefinitely: the point is that one of the characters is out of this weather, from this setting: he becomes a Big League player, but it is of this kind of man—strong, simple, full of earth and sun, and his life in relation to other lives that I want to write: I have got the man. I knew him as a child—he never made the Big League, but he could have. I mean, he would have looked real in a Big League uniform because, as I saw at the dinner, it was from just such fellows that the Big League players come. And I am not making the mistake of trying to write about him too professionally—too technically in relation to his merits as a player—I am simply trying to write about him as a living man.

The man was Jack Corbett. Wolfe knew Corbett around Ashville in 1915 and 1916 when the latter was managing the local club in the North Carolina League. Corbett recalls

Sandy Koufax receives the Babe Ruth Award as outstanding performer in the 1965 World Series. Presenting the plaque on behalf of the Baseball Writers' Association are Leonard Koppett of The New York Times and Jack Lane of The Long Island Press. *(Wide World)*

that Wolfe was "my batboy until we got in the park. Then he would shag a few flies during batting practice and disappear into the stands to watch the game." The park was about a mile from the now famous "Kentucky Home" where Wolfe lived. It had a wooden grandstand and bleachers holding about 1200 fans. The playing area was oddly built, short from left to center with a high fence, abnormally deep in right. On top of the fence was a large wooden bull, advertising Bull Durham tobacco. It was called Oates Park. Baseball men remember it because it was the scene of the shortest game ever played in

153

organized ball, a game that lasted 31 minutes. The strange contest, which almost certainly was witnessed by Wolfe, was a late-season meeting between Ashville and Winston-Salem, both out of the race, and was hurried to its conclusion by agreement so that the Winston-Salem players could catch a train. Everyone swung at the first pitch, which was lobbed up. Men over-ran bases in order to be tagged out. Once the pitcher was in such a hurry to get underway that he pitched to the batter while his opponents were still coming in from their fielding positions. The batter singled to center, raced around first, and tried to "stretch" the hit into a double. A teammate jogging toward the dugout grabbed the ball and tossed it to the second baseman for the out. This farce was already in the fourth inning before the umpire showed up, and the customers demanded and got their money back.

Jack Corbett was 5' 9½", weighed about 160, and could run well enough. A typical "good field, no hit" player, he never made the majors, although he did manage Ashville to a pennant in 1915. Wolfe turned to him whenever he wanted to describe a ballplayer. In Chapter 18 of *Look Homeward Angel*, Pearl Hines is thinking of marriage.

... Pearl juggled carefully with the proposals of several young men during this period. She had the warmest affection for a ball player, the second baseman and manager of the Altamont team. He was a tough, handsome young animal, forever hurling his glove down in a frenzy of despair during the course of a game, and rushing belligerently at the umpire. She liked his hard assurance, his rapid twang, his tanned, lean body.

But she was in love with no one—she would never be—and caution told her that the life-risk on bush-league ball-players was very great.

In Chapter 5 of *You Can't Go Home Again*, Corbett appears as Nebraska Crane. George Weber is on his way home to his aunt's funeral when he meets this boyhood friend long since a successful big league player. Crane, nearing the end of his career, still hopes to get a couple more seasons from a fading body.

Perhaps no passage in American fiction describes the feelings of a veteran professional athlete better than this ten-page conversation. At one point. Nebraska groans at George's mention of spring training. George, or Monk as Nebraska calls him, is amazed. "You mean you don't like it?" he asks.

"Like it! Them first three weeks is just plain hell. It ain't bad when you're a kid. You don't put on much weight durin' the winter, an' when you come down in the spring it only takes a few days to loosen up an' git the kinks out. In two weeks' time you're loose as ashes. But wait till you been aroun' as long as I have!" He laughed loudly and shook his head. "Boy! The first time you go after a grounder you can hear your joints creak. After a while you begin to limber up— you work into it an' git the soreness out of your muscles. By the time the season starts, along in April, you feel pretty good. By May you're goin' like a house a-fire, an' you tell yourself you're good as you ever was. You're still goin' strong along in June. An' then you hit July, an' you git them double-headers in St. Looie! Boy, oh boy!" Again he shook his head and laughed, baring big square teeth. "Monkus," he said quietly, turning to his companion, and now his face was serious and he had his black Indian look—"you ever been in St. Looie in July?"

"No."

"All right, then," he said very softly and scornfully. "An' you ain't played ball there in July. You come up to bat with sweat bustin' from your ears. You step up an' look out there to where the pitcher ought to be, an' you see four of him. The crowd in the bleachers is out there roastin' in their shirt-sleeves, an' when the pitcher throws the ball it just comes from nowheres—it comes right out of all them shirt-sleeves in the bleachers. It's on top of you before you know it. Well, anyway, you dig in an' git a toe-hold, take your cut, an' maybe you connect. You straighten out a fast one. It's good fer two bases if you hustle. In the old days you could've made it standin' up. But now —boy!" He shook his head slowly. "You can't tell me nothin' about

Four photos were combined to produce this
wide-angle "view from the bleachers" of Yankee
Stadium during the 1952 World Series. (Wide World)

that ball park in St. Looie in July! They got it all growed out in grass in April, but after July first"—he gave a short laugh—"hell!—it's paved with concrete! And when you git to first, them dogs is sayin', 'Boy, let's stay here!' But you gotta keep on goin'—you know the manager is watchin' you—you're gonna ketch hell if you don't take that extra base, it may mean the game. An' the boys up in the press box, they got their eyes glued on you, too—they've begun to say old Crane is playin' on a dime—an' you're thinkin about next year an' maybe gettin' in another Serious—an' you hope to God you don't git traded to St. Looie. So you take it on the lam, you slide into second like the Twentieth Century comin' into the Chicago yards—an' when you git up an' feel yourself all over to see if any of your parts is missin', you gotta listen to one of that second baseman's wisecracks: 'What's the hurry, Bras? Afraid you'll be late for the Vetrans' Reunion?' "

The conversation closes as the two men swap anecdotes and memories of their youth, Corbett's youth, Wolfe's youth.

"... I'll swear, Monk! I'm glad to see you!"

He put his big brown hand on his companion's knee. "It don't seem no time, does it? It all comes back!"

"Yes, Bras"—for a moment George looked out at the flashing land-scape with a feeling of sadness and wonder in his heart—"it all comes back."

The sadness and wonder were strong in James T. Farrell, too, who like his character Danny O'Neill gave up dreams of being a big-leaguer to write. I know what baseball has meant to James Farrell from Chicago's South Side. I have seen boys from lower middle-class neighborhoods, from the ghetto, coming by bus and subway to change their clothes in the bushes, to play on rocky fields with poor equipment and no recognition. I have seen them burst out upon the patchy grass, open, uncrowded, and felt their release—release from cramped rooms, cramped streets, cramped opportunities, from split families, drunken fathers, poverty, for the duration of a sandlot game. Farrell's stories may not be the greatest in American literature, but the baseball sections reach out to city dwellers who have been around the game.

His books are full with baseball. In fact, in 1957, he was able to assemble a whole volume of passages from his earlier works. Called *My Baseball Diary*, it is a nostalgic, sentimental collection drawn out of bitter sources. Naturally, much of *My Baseball Diary* is thinly veiled or out-

A young Chicago White Sox fan peers into the home team's dugout, program in hand. *(Wide World)*

right autobiography. One touching passage, entitled "My Grandmother Goes to Comiskey Park," is preceded by a personal reminiscence.

My grandmother is no more. She passed away in her sleep in 1931. I was raised by her and probably she wanted to see a baseball game because I was so full of baseball in my boyhood, and she most likely wondered what it was which interested her grandson, her son, Tom, and so many of the men.

She was born in County Westmeath, Ireland, and emigrated to America during the Civil War. . . . She never quite understood all the change that was going on in this country. Baseball was part of the excitement and strangeness of her new country. But once she saw a game, she wanted to see more, and as a little old woman, in her Sunday black dress, she went to ladies day alone in the early 1920's. Not telling anyone where she was going, she would dress up of a Friday afternoon and go to Comiskey Park on the street car. She came home excited. She liked to see the way the men would "lep" and run.

Baseball to her was part of the new world of America, but she saw it with the wonder of an unlettered peasant woman who had run the fields of Ireland as a girl in bare feet.

Even such an unlikely author as blues singer Bill Broonzy has left a "baseball" story. Broonzy was a Negro from the Deep South, rural Mississippi and Arkansas. Because he was a gifted singer and guitarist, he was able to leave the hopelessness of a world he never made to go north to the recording studios and concert stages of Chicago, New York, and Europe. By the time of his death on August 14, 1958, he was, in entertainment circles, a famous man. In 1953, disgusted after reading some of the literature that was being pumped out on the blues, he decided to do a book called *The Truth About the Blues*. Yannick Bruynoghe ultimately published the work as *Big Bill Blues: Big Bill Broonzy's Story as Told to Yannick Bruynoghe*.

In the introduction to the American edition, Bruynoghe states how Broonzy began his autobiography by writing "a series of short stories of all kinds." These are anecdotes that were eventually grouped under three headings: "My Life"; "My Songs"; "My Friends." Touched up though they have been in style, grammar, and structure, the narratives form a remarkable group of unsophisticated, straight-forward reports, full of opinion, folklore, and local color.

One of the 300-odd songs which Broonzy claimed to have written is called "Partnership Woman." It ends on an ancient note,

> Don't you never think your woman
> Just belongs to you
> I declare if she's sweet to you
> She'll be sweet to your partner too.

Broonzy's account of how "Partnership Woman" came to be composed is perhaps the best "story" he wrote. At the start he assures his reader that it is a true story,

... because I had a partner, and that's how we call a man when he and another love each other and that he would give him his clothes and his money and food. We call that a partner. I was raised with this man. I had known him all my life. . . . His name was Cicero Murphy.

The tale isn't very long. It tells how Bill "got together" with "this little woman, that we called Betty" and how he gives her money every week. Every two weeks, however, she takes off to see her cousin and aunt in the same town where Cicero works as a section-hand. Betty stays three or four days on Bill's money, comes back, sticks around till Bill is paid again, and repeats her trip. "She would just take the

Blues singer "Big Bill" Broonzy, who wrote the song "Partnership Woman" and described its genesis in a short story included in his autobiography. *(UPI)*

157

money and say: 'I'll be gone when you come back tonight, Bill.' "

The climax occurs on the Fourth of July when there is a big picnic that lasts four days. Both Cicero and Bill are off work and are to play for one of the baseball teams, Cicero to pitch, Bill to catch. Bill invites Betty to the picnic, not only to see him play, but to meet his "partner." Betty is noticeably reluctant, but she finally agrees to show up "later on." Even before the game, the battery-mates put two and two together and realize that they have a "partner-ship woman." They wait to see what she'll have to say. But "no Betty." As the game finishes, they find her watching from a tree, a secure perch from which she refuses to be lured. "Don't call her," advises Cicero, "I see her and I already know her as well as you do, my partner."

Bill goes home with his head hung, only to find Betty waiting for him and "looking as pretty as ever." A few feminine assurances along the lines of "Bill, it's you I love, not Cicero" and "I stay with you more than I do with him" rectify matters.

She kissed me and pulled her little arms around my neck.
"OK, Betty, you love me."

Cicero then shows up for dinner, and the three talk baseball rather than love. Bill concludes by saying,

Yes, that's how I thought up this song, by Betty making me and Cicero get along together, sleep with the same woman, and eat together.
After the picnic was over, Cicero went back to town and Betty would say to me:
"Can I go to see Cicero?"
"Yes," I'd say, "but don't stay too long . . .
And that's, I'm telling you, the real truth about the blues.

It is the "real truth" about baseball, too. The same sport which has integrated itself into the brave new world of the Irish immigrant grandmother has shown itself to be part of the ebb and flow of country Negro life, just as it was part of the ebb and flow of Thomas Wolfe's Carolina town life. For the fact of the matter is: in America, baseball is everywhere.

Because this game is a part of the fabric of our existence, citizens among us who have no real love for the game, who wouldn't play it if they could, are subtly compelled to respond to it. Think of Babbitt.

Baseball, Babbitt determined, would be an excellent hobby. "No sense a man's working his fool head off. I'm going to the Game three times a week. Besides, fellow ought to support the home team."
He did go and support the team, and enhance the glory of Zenith, by yelling "Attaboy!" and "Rotten!" He performed the rite scrupulously. He wore a cotton handkerchief about his collar; he became sweaty; he opened his mouth in a wide loose grin; and drank lemon soda out of a bottle. He went to the Game three times a week, for one week. Then he compromised on watching the *Advocate-Times* bulletin-board. He stood in the thickest and steamiest of the crowd, and as the boy up on the lofty platform recorded the achievements of Big Bill Bostwick, the pitcher, Babbitt remarked to complete strangers, "Pretty nice! Good work!" and hastened back to the office.
He honestly believed that he loved baseball. It is true that he hadn't, in twenty-five years, himself played any baseball except back-lot catch with Ted—very gentle, and strictly limited to ten minutes. But the game was a custom of his clan, and it gave outlet for the homicidal and sides-taking instincts which Babbitt called "patriotism" and "love of sport."

Serious writers are deeply aware of Babbitt. There's little point in John Keats' lines on the "sad heart of Ruth" as "she stood, in tears, amid the alien corn" if the reader doesn't know the *Old Testament*, less to Alexander Pope's advice, "Never gallop Pegasus to death," if the reader has forgotten his lessons in classical mythology. It's only when the Babbitts of "this favored land" acknowledge baseball that the game offers itself as a common ground on which our serious writers can meet our serious readers. So a poet like Rolfe Humphries will record his impressions of the Polo Grounds by writing,

> Time is of the essence. This is a highly skilled
> And beautiful mystery. Three or four seconds only
> From the time that Riggs connects till he reaches first,
> And in those seconds Jurges goes to his right,
> Comes up with the ball, tosses to Witek at second
> For the force on Reese, Witek to Mize at first,
> *In* time for the out—a double play.

—secure in the knowledge that his readers will respond to "the double play" as readily as John Steinbeck's readers will respond to "the grapes of wrath." So T. A. Daly can be confident that his dialect narration of "Da Greata Basaball" game between the Dagoman teams of Spolatro and Spagatti will bring a superior smile to 'Merican lips. And we see verified the fact that baseball is truly "a custom of our clan," as much a part of our heritage as "the Protestant ethic" or the state fair.

Somewhere, somehow, out of all this, an elusive dream has begun to take shape—a dream of using this national pastime to write the great national novel. The "forty-niners," the questers, have left a massive bibliography of baseball books along the way, a literature extending well beyond journalism and Ring Lardner, a literature that ranges all the way from Mark Twain's Arthurian knight sliding baseward like "an ironclad coming into port" to Bernard Malamud's complex association of "baseball mythology" and Jewish alienation.

It is tedious to sort through the literary heaps left

Bill Jurges at bat (above). Nicky Witek hauls one in (below).

159

New York's Polo Grounds are pictured in this 1887 lithograph appearing on the home game season schedule of the New York ball club. *(Culver Pictures)*

from this pursuit. For the most part the books can be separated into two piles. One is a group of sordid, "tough talk" tales which parallel in fiction the Jim Brosnan-Jim Bouton "dugout exposés" and which owe some part of their character to the "Buster tradition" of Lardner. The titles alone set the melody: Nelson Algren's *Never Come Morning*, Martin Quigley's *Today's Game*, Charles Einstein's *The Only Game in Town*, Eliot Asinof's *Man on Spikes*. The best are those by Professor Mark Harris: *The Southpaw*, *A Ticket for Seamstitch*, and *Bang the Drum Slowly*, the last featuring a catcher dying of Hodgkin's Disease, who loves an unscrupulous prostitute, and who relaxes by sitting in a hotel window trying to get curve on his spit. Perhaps the most extreme, and certainly the most satiric, is Robert Coover's *The Universal Baseball Association*, which deals with an accountant who has created a baseball game played with dice: a league, a schedule, players with personalities, a full set of statistics, attendance records, and receipts. The accountant, who lives in squalor over a delicatessen, is a boozy, lecherous fellow and continually mixes his imaginary game and its boozy, lecherous participants with his real life. Red Smith, who didn't like the novel, remarked in *Book World* that ". . . a little fantasy goes a long way . . . and after an imaginary beanball kills an imaginary player named Damon Rutherford, the author never finds the strike zone again."

A little fantasy does go a long way, but this fact has not kept a second group of light-hearted, often lightheaded, baseball tales from their genesis. For the national game has managed to bring out the worst in otherwise talented comic writers. Lardner certainly proved that one doesn't need midgets scurrying down the first baseline, tomcats who inherit teams, crack-pot millionaires who bequeath the White Sox to the Russians, or financiers who hope to control all the dogs in the world to write funny books about baseball. Yet works that use these ideas, works like James Thurber's *You Could Look It Up*, H. Allen Smith's *Rhubarb*, Paul Malloy's *A Pennant for the Kremlin*, and Kenneth Koch's mock epic poem *Ko, or A Season on Earth*, all tend to stress eccentricity or "the cute," their authors feeling, I suppose, that a game ungarnished must be inadequate. Even the best of the lot, Heywood Broun's *The Sun Field*, suffers from this fever. It climaxes with a scene in which the Babe Ruth-like hero holds a statue-like pose in the outfield as the Series-winning run crosses the plate, simply because his wife has remarked, "When you draw back your arm to throw the line is as fine as anything in Greek sculpture."

But the point is the American writers are "in there, swinging away," and authors like Coover and Koch are using the most sophisticated narrative techniques known to our literature. Sooner or later one of them is going to connect and the classical baseball book will happen.

Irwin Shaw might have been the one in his *Voices of a Summer Day*, a novel in which he uses a baseball game as a catalyst. A father, Benjamin Federov, is watching his 13-year-old boy play centerfield in a Long Island beach town. As he sits there in the summer sun . . .

Dozing, almost alone on the rows of benches, one game slid into other games, other generations were at play many years before . . . in Harrison, New Jersey, where he had grown up; on college campuses, where he had never been quite good enough to make the varsity, despite his fleetness of foot and sure-handedness in the field. The sounds were the same through the years—the American sounds of

Gerald Ford, then House Majority Leader, and longtime Speaker of the House John McCormack watch Washington Senators manager Ted Williams demonstrate batting grip prior to the 1969 Congressional Democrats vs. Republicans game, which traditionally precedes a Senators-Orioles contest each year. *(Wide World)*

summer, the tap of bat against ball, the cries of the infielders, the wooden plump of the ball into catchers' mitts, the umpires calling "Strike three and you're out." The generations circled the bases, the dust rose for forty years as runners slid in from third, dead boys hit doubles, famous men made errors at shortstop, forgotten friends tapped the clay from their spikes with their bats as they stepped into the batter's box, coaches' voices warned, across the decades, "Tag up, tag up!" on fly balls. The distant, mortal innings of boyhood and youth . . .

But the story is not really about baseball, it is about a Jewish youngster growing up in New Jersey, and while Shaw returns from time to time to the game, one is perfectly aware that football or basketball or a piece of cake would have served him as well. Furthermore, the book has received little acclaim.

Bernard Malamud might have been another. In *The Natural*, Malamud tells the story of Roy Hobbs, leftfielder, owner of the magic bat Wonderboy, and of his experiences as a star for the New York Knights. Hobbs, whose role in baseball's "mythology" is supposed to suggest Achilles' role in Greek mythology and Sir Percival's role in the Arthuriad, has a diamond-shaped world-view which is limited by baseball and the heroism attainable there.

"What will you hope to accomplish, Roy?"

He had already told her but after a minute remarked, "Sometimes when I walk down the street I bet people will say there goes Roy Hobbs, the best there ever was in the game."

She gazed at him with touched and troubled eyes. "Is that all?"

He tried to penetrate her question. Twice he had answered it and still she was unsatisfied. He couldn't be sure what she expected him to say. "Is that all?" he repeated. "What more is there?"

"Don't you know?" . . .

"Isn't there something over and above earthly things—some more glorious meaning to one's life and activities?"

"In baseball?"

At the end of the book, as Roy Hobbs lies sick and confused in a hospital bed, he sees the world beyond baseball for the first time. Told by the doctor that he must give up the game or suffer a heart attack, told by his latest girlfriend that she can be made only by men who first make the kind of money baseball stars make, Hobbs is tempted by the owner of the Knights to throw a play-off game. He succumbs, leaving the world of "baseball mythology" and entering reality. When in the midst of the game, he recants and tries to re-enter the "mythology" he has left, he finds that "you can't go home again." Wonderboy, the magic bat, shatters. He has nothing to do but collect the bribe and "defrocked" enter everyday mediocrity, reveal-ing his frustration by beating up the owner and the bookie who have "fixed" him and showering the money he has received over the owner's head. "He coulda been a king," a woman comments as he passes by old, grimy, and unshaven.

Robert Taubman reviewing Shaw's *Voices of a Summer Day* in the *New Statesman* said it was "no more than a pop-up." Perhaps that is fair; perhaps the comment would cover *The Natural* and Coover's and Harris's works, too. But remember—"they're getting a piece of it" . . . And one of these days! . . .

So if the dream has proved elusive, if that *one* baseball book remains unpublished, the pursuit clearly shows that there is nothing inherent in "a boy's game" to prevent a great writer from using it as a vehicle for a masterpiece. Bad, indifferent, good, but never great, the works of the last forty years offer a steady denial to F. Scott Fitzgerald's comment that baseball has "no more possibilities in it than a boy could master." They reflect the far more astute opinion of Virginia Woolf that baseball offers the writer the same sort of focal point that society offers British writers. After all, if Henry James, Anthony Trollope, Jane Austen, and others like them can attain firm places in literary history by seeing the "possibilities" of an "international episode," a vicarage, a hedged home, then someone will see the same in "a boy's game." It's just, in Thoreau's words, a matter of finding the writer who will travel "widely in Concord." For Mudville's Caedmon must inevitably appear—some frustrated ballplayer, perhaps, who wanders away from the annual dinner of the Baseball Writers Association to be touched in his sleep by an angel, awakening to "make the masters in their turn his hearers"!

INDEX

II. OTHER PERSONS
(excepting folk heroes)

III. TITLES OF IMPORTANT BOOKS, POEMS, AND THE LIKE

IV. GENERAL TOPICS

INDEX